© Copyrig

All rights Reserved. No pa
in it may be quoted from ᴏ
such as printing, scanning, photocopying or otherwise without prior written permission of the copyright holder.

Disclaimer and Terms of Use: Effort has been made to ensure that the information in this book is accurate and complete, however, the author and the publisher do not warrant the accuracy of the information, text and graphics contained within the book due to the rapidly changing nature of science, research, known and unknown facts and internet. The Author and the publisher do not hold any responsibility for errors, omissions or contrary interpretation of the subject matter herein. This book is presented solely for motivational and informational purposes only.

Table of Contents

Introduction **9**
About Instant Pot **10**
The benefits of Instant Pot **11**
Measurement conversions **12**
Useful Tips **13**
    Include in The Daily Diet and Stay Healthy 13
Grains Recipes **14**
    Peaches & Cream Oatmeal (S&F) 15
    Creamy Banana Oatmeal (S&F) 16
    Breakfast Quinoa (S&F) 17
    Buckwheat Porridge (S&F) 18
    Apple and Spiced Lentils (VEG) 19
    Perfect Quinoa (VEG) 20
    Cranberry-Almond Quinoa (VEG, S&F) 21
    Creamy Strawberry Rolled Oats 22
    Apple Spice Oats (VEG) 23
    Steel-Cut Oats (S&F) 24
    Pear Oats with Walnuts (VEG, S&F) 25
    Stewed Chickpeas 26
Rice Recipes **27**
    White Rice (VEG, S&F) 28
    Brown Rice (VEG, S&F) 29
    Brown Rice Medley (VEG) 30
    Mexican Rice (VEG) 31
    Mexican Casserole (VEG) 32
    Delicious Risotto 33

Mushroom and Pea Risotto 34

Butter Rice (S&F) 35

Vegetable Cajun Rice (VEG) 36

Fried Rice 38

Cauliflower Rice (VEG) 39

Bean Recipes 40

Steamed Green Beans 40

Black Bean + Sweet Potato Hash (VEG) 41

White Bean Dip with Tomatoes (VEG) 42

Baked Beans 43

Beans Stew (VEG) 44

Stewed Tomatoes and Green Beans (VEG) 45

Three Bean Salad (VEG) 46

Red Beans (VEG) 48

Chili Con Carne 50

Poultry Recipes 51

The Whole Chicken (S&F) 51

Sticky Sesame Chicken (S&F) 52

Buttery Chicken 53

Salsa Verde Chicken (S&F) 55

Balsamic Chicken Thighs 56

Italian Chicken 57

Chicken Noodle 58

Hot Buffalo Wings 60

Creamy Chicken and Mushroom 62

Chicken BBQ 64

Honey-Sriracha Chicken 66

Turkey Verde and Rice (S&F)...... 67

Turkey Drumsticks...... 68

Stuffed Turkey Tenderloin 69

Thanksgiving Turkey Casserole 71

Egg Recipes 72

Hard-Boiled Eggs (S&F) 72

Soft-Boiled Egg (S&F) 73

Delightful Soft Eggs 74

French Toast Bake 75

Poached Tomato Eggs 76

Scrambled Eggs (S&F) 77

Aromatic Bacon Eggs 78

Cheesy Sausage Frittata 79

Savory Breakfast Egg Porridge 80

Beef Recipes 81

Marinated Steak 81

Beef Stroganoff 82

Garlic Teriyaki Beef 83

Beef And Broccoli 84

Italian Beef 85

Korean Beef 86

Beef Short Ribs 87

Beefy Lasagna 88

Balsamic Maple Beef 90

Mississippi Pot Roast 91

Instant Pot Roast 92

Teriyaki Short Ribs 93

Sweet-Spicy Meatloaf 94

Texas-Style Beef Chili 95

Swedish Meatballs 96

Pork and Lamb Recipes 97

Teriyaki Pork Tenderloin 97

Pork Ribs BBQ 98

Honey Pork Chops 99

Pork Chops With Mushroom Gravy 100

Pork Fried Rice 101

Pork Carnitas 102

Pork Cutlets With the Plum Sauce 104

Cilantro Pork Tacos 105

Pork Satay 106

Pulled pork 107

Ham and Peas (S&F) 108

Thyme Lamb (S&F) 109

Lamb Shanks 110

Lamb and Avocado Salad 112

Seafood Recipes 113

Quick Seafood Paella 113

Seafood Cranberries Plov 115

Shrimp Creole 116

Grispy Skin Salmon Fillet 117

Dijon Salmon (S&F) 118

Tuna and Pasta Casserole 119

Fish in Orange Ginger Sauce 120

Wild Alaskan Cod In The Pot 121

Cod Chowder...122

Tilapia bites 124

Spicy Lemony Salmon 125

Soup Recipes...**126**

Simple Chicken Soup...127

Chicken Tortilla Soup 128

Bean Soup 129

Spiced-Carrot Chilled Soup (VEG) 130

Cheddar Broccoli and Potato Soup 131

Split Pea Soup (VEG, S&F) 132

Sweet Potato Soup (VEG) 133

Quinoa Soup (VEG, S&F) 134

Turkish Soup..135

Vegetable Recipes **136**

Breakfast Potato Hash (VEG)...137

Baked Potatoes (VEG, S&F) 138

Sweet Potatoes (VEG, S&F) 139

Garlicky Mashed Potatoes 140

Coconut Butter Garlic New Potatoes (VEG) 141

Steamed Broccoli (VEG) 142

Pumpkin Puree (VEG)..143

Zucchini and Mushrooms (VEG)..144

Ricotta-Stuffed Zucchini 145

Brussels Sprouts (VEG, S&F) 146

Eggplant With Carrots, Tomatoes, and Bell Peppers 147

Spaghetti Squash (VEG)..148

Sweet and Sour Red Cabbage (VEG) 149

Ratatouille (VEG) 150

Polenta with Fresh Herbs (VEG) 151

Mushroom Gravy (VEG) 152

Broccoli Pesto (VEG) 153

Sweet And Sour Red Cabbage (VEG) 154

Stocks and Sauces 155

Chicken Stock 155

Beef Bone Broth 157

Bone Broth 158

Meat Sauce 159

Vegetable Stock (VEG) 160

Tomato Sauce (VEG) 161

Mushroom Sauce (VEG) 162

Cranberry Apple Sauce (VEG) 163

Tabasco Sauce 164

Dessert Recipes 165

Apple Crisp 166

Cranberry Apple Steel Cut Oats 167

Baked Apples (VEG) 168

Carrot Cake Breakfast Oatmeal 169

Lemon-Ruby Pears (VEG) 170

Chocolate Cheesecake 171

Cashew-Lemon Cheesecake 172

Cranberry-Pear Cake 174

Stewed Pears (VEG) 175

Rich and Creamy Rice Pudding 176

Pears Stewed in Red Wine (VEG) 177

Mango Cake 178

Chocolate Fondue 179

Blueberry Pudding 180

Pumpkin-Spice Brown Rice Pudding with Dates (VEG) 181

Tapioca with Fresh Berries (VEG) 182

Introduction

The book presented to you is a collection of recipes of various and incredibly delicious dishes. Here everyone will find something to their taste. The author of this book has selected for you the best easy and the tasty recipes of dishes made in a pressure cooker Instant Pot.

Using this book, you will get some advantages:

- You will be able to choose a remarkably delicious dish both for yourself and for the whole family.
- You will find many recipes for vegetarians in a special section or marked as VEG in other sections.
- Most recipes are **SET&FORGET**, marked with an S&F sign. **It means that the recipes are simple and very easy.**
- You will know the exact proportions of the ingredients and the cooking time of each dish.
- You will get a step-by-step instruction on making each dish in an Instant Pot.
- Useful tips and secrets of how to make dishes even tastier.
- And lots of other helpful information.

Eat with pleasure, creating a pleasant atmosphere for digesting, if possible.

About Instant Pot

- Instant Pot does the same thing that seven kitchen appliances would do. It functions as an electric pressure cooker, as a slow cooker, as a rice cooker, as a yogurt maker, as a steamer, as a warming pot and as a browning or sauté pan. Same functionality, better reliability!
- Instant Pot has a 24 hour delayed cooking timer option that can be programmed for perfect meal planning.
- Instant Pot is very convenient; you can set the Instant Pot and leave to attend to your other house chores.
- It is relatively affordable for a house hold appliance with lots of functionality.
- The Instant Pot's time saving ability is out of this world when used to cook meals and recipes with lentils, dried beans, stews and grains as ingredients.
- The Instant Pot is built to last and it is made from stainless steel, so it's very easy to clean.
- The Instant Pot is that appliance that you get a grip on with minimal reading of manufacturer's manual; with a little time spent reading the manual, you are ready to start cooking.
- Cooking meals like rice and steel cut oats takes time when using a stovetop cooker and a lot of planning when compared to the very-easy-to-use Instant Pot. It is super fast, user friendly and reliable.
- The more you use the Instant Pot, the more you get used to it.
- The more you use it to cook different meals, the more easy to use it becomes and the more discoveries you make of the several ways to use the Instant Pot.

The benefits of Instant Pot

Convenient: 16 turn-key function keys for the most common cooking tasks. Planning the meal with delayed cooking up to 24 hours, reducing cooking time by up to 70%.

Cooking healthy, nutritious and tasty meals: smart programming for delicious healthy food, consistent every time.

Clean & Pleasant: absolutely quiet, no steam, no smell, no spills, no excessive heat in the kitchen. 6-in-1 capability reduces clutter in the kitchen.

Energy efficient: saves up to 70% of energy.

Safe and dependable: Instant Pot is UL/ULC certified UL Logo Instant Pot and has 10 fool-proof safety protections.

Measurement conversions

Use it for accurate measuring of the necessary ingredients.

Metric to standard	Fahrenheit to Celsius	Cups to tablespoons	Oz to grams
5 ml = 1 tsp	300 F = 150 C	3 tsp = 1 tbsp	1 oz = 29 g
15 ml = 1 tbsp	350 F = 180 C	1/8 cup = 2 tbsp	2 oz = 57 g
30 ml = 1 fluid oz	375 F = 190 C	1/4 cup = 4 tbsp	3 oz = 85 g
240 ml = 1 cup	400 F = 200 C	1/3 cup = 5 tbsp + 1 tsp	4 oz = 113 g
1 liter = 34 fluid oz	425 F = 220 C		5 oz = 142 g
1 liter = 4.2 cups	450 F = 230 C	1/2 cup = 8 tbsp	6 oz = 170 g
1 gram = .035 oz		3/4 cup = 12 tbsp	7 oz = 198 g
100 grams = 3.5 oz		1 cup = 16 tbsp	8 oz = 227 g
500 grams = 1.10 lb		8 fluid oz = 1 cup	10 oz = 283 g
		1 pint 2 cups = 16 fluid oz	20 oz = 567 g
			30 oz = 850 g
		1 quart 2 pints = 4 cups	40 oz = 1133 g
		1 gallon 4 quarts = 16 cups	

Abbreviations

oz = ounce

fl oz = fluid ounce

tsp = teaspoon

tbsp = tablespoon

ml = milliliter

c = cup

pt = pint

qt = quart

gal = gallon

L = liter

Useful Tips

Include in The Daily Diet and Stay Healthy

Optimizing your metabolism is the key to weight loss (a high metabolism means you burn calories even at rest, making all lazy people's dreams come true).

Boosting your metabolism is also critical for many other bodily functions related to maintaining general health.

A strong metabolism is tied to more than a svelte body - it's beneficial for immune function, lower rates of infectious and degenerative diseases, fertility and a healthy sex drive, lean muscle mass, having more energy and vigor, brain functionality, longevity, and much more.

Grains Recipes

Peaches & Cream Oatmeal (S&F)

(Prep + Cook Time: 20 minutes | Servings: 4)

This oatmeal recipe is great for when that stone fruit is in season, but you can easily substitute with strawberries or other seasonal beauties.

Ingredients:

2 cups rolled oats

4 cups water

1 tsp vanilla

1 chopped peach

Optional:

½ cup chopped almonds

2 tbsp flax meal

Splash of cream, milk

Maple syrup

Directions:

1. Combine the water, peaches, oats, and vanilla in the Instant Pot.
2. Set to HIGH pressure using the PORRIDGE setting. Be sure the valve is sealed. Adjust the time to three minutes.
3. Allow the pressure to release naturally for ten minutes; then perform a quick release for the remainder of the pressure.
4. Garnish as desired and enjoy

Nutritional Info (per serving): Calories – 168; Fat - 2.7; Fiber – 4.5; Carbs – 30.2; Protein – 5.6

Creamy Banana Oatmeal (S&F)

(Prep + Cook Time: 25 minutes | Servings: 4)

Make this awesome oatmeal with steel-cut oats. It's a very rich-tasting oatmeal thanks to the half-and-half, so feel free to eat this cold for a quick dessert later if you have any leftovers.

Ingredients:

2 ¼ cups water

½ cup steel-cut oats

2 very ripe, chopped bananas

½ cup packed light brown sugar

¼ cup half-and-half

2 tsp vanilla extract

½ tsp ground cinnamon

¼ tsp salt

Directions:

1. Mix oats, bananas, brown sugar, vanilla, salt, and cinnamon with 2 ¼ cups and pour into the Instant Pot.
2. When the brown sugar dissolves, close the lid.
3. Select MANUAL and then 18 minutes at HIGH pressure.
4. When time is up, press CANCEL and wait for the pressure to come down on its own.
5. When time is up, carefully open the cooker.
6. Stir in the half-and half, and enjoy!

Nutritional Info (per serving): Calories - 130; Fat - 3; Fiber - 2; Carbs - 26; Protein - 3

Breakfast Quinoa (S&F)

(Prep + Cook Time: 10 minutes | Servings: 6)

This very fast quinoa recipe for breakfast is low in saturated fat, has no cholesterol, low in sodium, very high in magnesium, and very high in phosphorus.

Ingredients:

2 ¼ cups water

1 ½ cups quinoa, uncooked, well rinsed

2 tbsp maple syrup

½ tsp vanilla Pinch salt

¼ tsp ground cinnamon

Optional toppings:

Fresh berries

Milk

Sliced almonds

Directions:

1. Put all of the ingredients into the Instant Pot and close the lid.
2. Set the pressure to HIGH and the timer to 1 minute.
3. When the timer beeps, turn the Instant Pot off, let the pressure release for 10 minutes naturally and then turn the steam valve to release remaining pressure.
4. Carefully open the lid.
5. Fluff the cooked quinoa.
6. Serve with berries, milk, and almonds.

Nutritional Info (per serving): Calories - 175; Fat – 2.6; Fiber - 3; Carbs – 31.9; Protein - 6

Buckwheat Porridge (S&F)

(Prep + Cook Time: 35 minutes | Servings: 4)

This gluten-free vegan breakfast porridge is creamy like rice pudding. Each serving has no cholesterol, very low in saturated fat, low in sodium, and high in manganese.

Ingredients:

1 banana, sliced

1 cup raw buckwheat groats

1 tsp ground cinnamon

½ tsp vanilla

¼ cup raisins

3 cups milk

Chopped nuts, optional

Directions:

1. Rinse the buckwheat and then put in the Instant Pot container.
2. Add the rice milk, raisins, banana, vanilla, and cinnamon. Close the lid and make sure the valve is closed.
3. Set to MANUAL, the pressure is HIGH, and the timer to 6 minutes. When the timer beeps at the end of the cooking cycle, unplug the pot, and let the pressure release on natural for about 20 minutes.
4. With a long handled spoon, stir the porridge.
5. Divide the porridge between 4 bowls.
6. Add more milk into each serving to desired consistency. If desired, sprinkle with chopped nuts.

Nutritional Info (per serving): Calories - 247; Fat – 2.6; Fiber – 4.4; Carbs – 54.3; Protein – 4.7

Apple and Spiced Lentils (VEG)

(Prep + Cook Time: 30 minutes | Servings: 4)

Spiced lentils perfectly balanced with the sweetness of maple syrup and unique flavors of apple is a healthy breakfast that will keep you charged for the day.

Ingredients:

1 cup red lentils, soaked for 30 minutes
2 medium-sized apples, cored
1 tbsp ground cinnamon
1 tsp turmeric powder
¼ tsp ground cinnamon
1 tsp ground cloves
1 tbsp maple syrup
1 cup coconut milk, divided
3 cups red rooibos tea, brewed

Directions:

1. Drain lentils and place in a 6-quarts Instant Pot along with remaining ingredients except for maple syrup and milk.
2. Stir until combine, then plug in and switch on the Instant Pot.
3. Secure pot with lid, then position PRESSURE indicator and adjust cooking time on timer pad to 2 minutes and let cook. Instant Pot will take 10 minutes to build pressure before cooking timer starts.
4. When the timer beeps, switch off the Instant Pot and let pressure release naturally for 10 minutes and then do quick pressure release.
5. Then uncover the pot, stir until well mixed and then divide equally among serving bowl.
6. Serve with a generous amount of milk and maple syrup.

Nutritional Info (per serving): Calories - 168; Fat - 1; Fiber - 11; Carbs - 34; Protein - 9

Perfect Quinoa (VEG)

(Prep + Cook Time: 15 minutes | Servings: 4)

Quinoa is a great side dish idea. It contains all of the nine amino acids. It's also a great source of magnesium, potassium, phosphorus, and manganese. It has a wonderfully unique texture and can be served with many dishes.

Ingredients:

2 cups quinoa (any color)

3 cups vegetable (or chicken) broth or water

2 pinches salt

Juice of one lemon

Handful your choice of fresh herbs, minced

Directions:
1. Rinse the quinoa well.
2. Preferably, you should soak it overnight in filtered water mixed with 1 tablespoon apple cider vinegar or lemon juice.
3. Strain and put into the Instant Pot. Add the broth, lemon juice, salt, and, if using, herbs.
4. Close and lock the lid. Press MANUAL and set the time to 1 minute.
5. When the timer beeps, let the pressure release naturally for 10 minutes.
6. Turn the steam valve to VENTING. Carefully open the lid and serve the quinoa.

Nutritional Info (per serving): Calories - 344; Fat – 6.2; Fiber – 0.7; Carbs - 6; Protein – 15.7

Cranberry-Almond Quinoa (VEG, S&F)

(Prep + Cook Time: 10 minutes | Servings: 4)

The vegans aren't the only ones who will adore this easy side dish. It's perfect for the holidays when cranberries are a common ingredient, and there's a lot of beautiful crunch thanks to the almonds and sunflower seeds.

Ingredients:

2 cups water

1 cup quinoa

1 cup dried cranberries

½ cup slivered almonds

¼ cup salted sunflower seeds

Directions:

1. Rinse quinoa before putting in the pot with water.
2. Seal the lid. Press the MANUAL key and adjust time to 10 minutes.
3. When time is up, press STOP and quick-release the pressure.
4. Mix in sunflower seeds, almonds, and dried cranberries.
5. Serve.

Nutritional Info (per serving): Calories - 383; Fat - 9; Fiber – 7.5; Carbs - 66; Protein - 8

Creamy Strawberry Rolled Oats

(Prep + Cook Time: 20 minutes | Servings: 2)

Skip the instant version oatmeal of this recipe that don't actually contain any cream or strawberries. With an Instant Pot, you can cook it with real ingredients. This oat dish is high in manganese, phosphorus, and selenium.

Ingredients:

2/3 cup whole milk

2 tbsp strawberries, freeze-dried (or your favorite dried or frozen fruit)

1/3 cup rolled oats

½ tsp white sugar

1 pinch salt

Directions:

1. Pour 2 cups of water into the Instant Pot container and then put a steamer basket or a rack with a handle in the pot.
2. In a small-sized, heat-safe mug or bowl, add the oats, strawberries, milk, and salt.
3. Close and lock the pot lid. Set the pressure to high and the timer to 10 minutes.
4. When the timer beeps, unplug the pot. Let the pressure release for about 7-10 minutes naturally or until the pressure indicator is down and then open the lid. You can turn the steam valve to release remaining pressure before opening. Carefully remove the mug/ bowl from the pot.
5. Mix the contents vigorously and then sprinkle with sugar to taste. Serve.

Nutritional Info (per serving): Calories - 214; Fat – 7.1; Fiber – 3.1; Carbs – 29.2; Protein – 8.9

Apple Spice Oats (VEG)

(Prep + Cook Time: 10 minutes | Servings: 2)

Sweetened with a fresh apple, these vegan steel-cut oats are perfect for chilly fall mornings, or any time you feel like waking up with a hit of sweet-spiciness.

Ingredients:

1 ½ cups almond milk

1 peeled and chopped apple

½ cup steel-cut oats

1 tsp ground cinnamon

Dash of nutmeg

Directions:

1. Put everything in your Instant Pot and seal the lid.
2. Hit MANUAL and cook for just 4 minutes.
3. When time is up, hit CANCEL and wait for a natural pressure release.
4. Stir and serve!

Nutritional Info (per serving): Calories - 255; Fat - 4; Fiber - 5; Carbs - 39; Protein - 5

Steel-Cut Oats (S&F)

(Prep + Cook Time: 10 minutes | Servings: 4)

Oats are one of the best breakfasts you could have. They're full of fiber, so a bowl keeps you full till lunchtime, so you aren't snacking your way through the morning. If you've been making oats in the microwave or waiting by the stovetop, you'll be overjoyed at the speed and quality of the Instant Pot's steel-cut oatmeal.

Ingredients:

2 cups of water

1 cup steel-cut oats

Pinch of salt

Milk

Sugar

Directions:

1. Pour 1 cup of water into the Instant Pot and lower in the trivet.
2. In a heatproof bowl, mix 2 cups of water, oats, and salt.
3. Set on top of the trivet and lock the pressure cooker lid.
4. Select the MANUAL setting and cook for at least 6 minutes, but no more than 7.
5. Heat a cup or so of milk (depending on how much you want) in the microwave.
6. When the oats are done, scoop into individual serving bowls.
7. Pour milk on top and add sugar before serving.

Nutritional Info (per serving): Calories -155 ; Fat - 3; Fiber - 23; Carbs - 28; Protein - 4

Pear Oats with Walnuts (VEG, S&F)

(Prep + Cook Time: 10 minutes | Servings: 4)

The oats cook in almond milk, sugar, and just a tablespoon of coconut oil. Fresh pears will soften beautifully in there, as well, and you finish it off with cinnamon and walnuts.

Ingredients:

2 cups almond milk

2 cups peeled and cut pears

1 cup rolled oats

½ cup chopped walnuts

¼ cup sugar

1 tbsp melted coconut oil

¼ tsp salt

Dash of cinnamon

Directions:

1. Mix everything except the walnuts and cinnamon in an oven-safe bowl that you know fits in the Instant Pot.
2. Pour 1 cup of water into the pressure cooker and lower in steamer rack.
3. Put the bowl on top and lock the lid. Select MANUAL and then HIGH pressure for 6 minutes.
4. When time is up, quick-release the pressure.
5. Carefully remove the bowl, divide into 4 servings, and season with salt and cinnamon.

Nutritional Info (per serving): Calories - 288; Fat - 13; Fiber – 4.5; Carbs - 39; Protein - 5

Stewed Chickpeas

(Prep + Cook Time: 45 minutes | Servings: 4)

This recipe is very easy and the preparation is simple. This flavorful dish is saucy because of the tomato puree, which adds sweetness to offset the smoked paprika.

Ingredients:

1 ½ tbsp smoked paprika
1 jar (680 grams or 24 ounces) tomatoes, strained
½ tsp ground cumin
½ tsp rounded sea salt
1/8-1/4 tsp ground allspice
2 cans chickpeas (14 or 15 ounces each rinsed and drained)
2 large-sized or
3 small-sized-medium-sized onions, chopped (about 3-3 1/2 cups)
2/3 cup dates, pitted, chopped
2-3 tbsp water, more as needed

Directions:

1. Press the SAUTE key of the Instant Pot.
2. Add the onions, cumin, paprika, salt, and allspice.
3. Cook for about 6 to 7 minutes, occasionally stirring, adding more water if sticking.
4. Add the tomatoes, chickpeas, and dates, and stir until mixed through. Press the CANCEL key to stop the sauté function. Cover and lock the lid.
5. Press the MANUAL key, set the pressure to HIGH, and set the timer for 20 minutes.
6. When the Instant Pot timer beeps, press the CANCEL key. Turn the steam valve to quick release the pressure.
7. Alternatively, you can naturally release the pressure. Unlock and carefully open the lid.
8. Stir and mix through and, if desired, add seasoning.
9. Serve over cooked whole-grain, such with quinoa, millet, and brown rice.
10. You can also serve over mashed potatoes, roasted squash, and steamed kale.

Notes: Use jarred strained tomatoes – it gives a better texture than crushed tomatoes and lets the base cook down to a more uniform sauce.

Nutritional Info (per serving): Calories - 867; Fat – 12.9; Fiber – 41.1; Carbs - 156; Protein – 41.6

Rice Recipes

White Rice (VEG, S&F)

(Prep + Cook Time: 15 minutes | Servings: 4)

If you are a first timer and you don't know the tricks and tips about cooking rice, it can end up mushy or burnt. This is a foolproof way to cook rice – it comes out perfect every time!

Ingredients:

1 cup white basmati rice

1 cup water

Directions:

1. Put the rice in a colander.
2. Rinse until the water is clear.
3. Transfer into the Instant Pot and then add the water.
4. Set the pot to MANUAL, set the pressure to LOW, and the timer to 8 minutes.
5. When the timer beeps, quick release the pressure.
6. Fluff the rice using a fork and serve.

Nutritional Info (per serving): Calories - 225; Fat – 0.4; Fiber – 0.8; Carbs – 49.3; Protein – 4.4

Brown Rice (VEG, S&F)

(Prep + Cook Time: 30 minutes | Servings: 6)

Nutty-flavored and dense-textured brown rice made healthier when you cook it with fish broth, which is high in selenium.

Ingredients:

2 cups brown rice

½ tsp of sea salt

2 ½ cups any kind vegetable broth or water

Directions:

1. Put the rice into the Instant Pot.
2. Pour in the broth or water and salt. Close and lock the lid. Press the MANUAL and set the timer to 22 minutes pressure cooking.
3. When the timer beeps, naturally release the pressure for 10 minutes.
4. Carefully open the lid. Serve.

Nutritional Info (per serving): Calories - 245; Fat – 2.3; Fiber – 2.1; Carbs – 48.6; Protein – 6.8

Brown Rice Medley (VEG)

(Prep + Cook Time: 35 minutes | Servings: 4)

What's better than cooking perfect brown rice in the Instant Pot? Cooking a medley of rice, of course!

Ingredients:

2-4 tbsp red, wild or black rice

¾ cup (or more) short grain brown rice

1 ½ cups water

1 tbsp water

3/8-1/2 tsp sea salt, optional

Directions:

1. Put as much as 2-4 tablespoons of red, wild, or black rice or use all three kinds in 1-cup measuring cup.
2. Add brown rice to make 1 cup total of rice. Put the rice in a strainer and wash. Put the rice in the Instant Pot.
3. Add 1 1/2 cup plus 1 tablespoon water in the pot. If desired, add salt.
4. Stir and then check the sides of the pot to make sure the rice is pushed down into the water. Close and lock the lid. Press MULTIGRAIN and set the time to 23 minutes.
5. When the timer beeps, let the pressure release naturally for 5 minutes, then turn the steam valve and release the pressure slowly.
6. If you have time, let the pressure release naturally for 15 minutes. Stir and serve.

Nutritional Info (per serving): Calories - 165; Fat – 1.1; Fiber – 1.8; Carbs – 34.6; Protein – 4.1

Mexican Rice (VEG)

(Prep + Cook Time: 35 minutes | Servings: 6)

This recipe is a foolproof way to make Mexican rice using white or brown rice. Pair with beans, soup, or meat dish.

Ingredients:

2 cups rice, long-grain, such as Lundberg Farms Brown Basmati

½ cup tomato paste

½ white onion, chopped

2 cups water

2 tsp salt

3 cloves garlic, minced

1 small jalapeño, optional

Directions:

1. Set the Instant Pot to normal SAUTE. Heat the olive oil.
2. Add the garlic, onion, rice, and salt. Sauté for about 3-4 minutes or until fragrant.
3. Mix the tomato paste with the water until well combined. Pour into the pot. Add the whole jalapeno pepper.
4. Press CANCEL. Close and lock the lid. Press PRESSURE, set to HIGH, and the timer for 3 minutes is using white rice or for 22 minutes if using brown rice.
5. When the timer beeps, release the pressure naturally for about 15 minutes. Turn the steam valve to VENTING. Carefully open the lid.
6. Using a fork, fluff the rice and serve hot.

Nutritional Info (per serving): Calories - 253; Fat – 1.8; Fiber – 3.3; Carbs – 53.7; Protein – 5.9

Mexican Casserole (VEG)

(Prep + Cook Time: 35 minutes | Servings: 4)

Get ready to make the easiest casserole ever. You just need rice, beans, tomato paste, and a few spices. It's a great option for when you're trying to put off going to the store, but you don't want to eat a dinner of crackers and peanut butter.

Ingredients:

5 cups water

2 cups uncooked brown rice

1 cup soaked black beans

6 oz tomato paste

2 tsp chili powder

2 tsp onion powder

1 tsp garlic

1 tsp salt

Directions:

1. A few hours before dinner, put your dry beans in a bowl with enough water to cover them.
2. Soak on the countertop for at least two hours and drain.
3. Put everything in your Instant Pot. Close and seal the pressure cooker. Select MANUAL and then cook on HIGH pressure for 28 minutes.
4. When time is up, hit CANCEL and quick-release.
5. Taste and season more if necessary.

Nutritional Info (per serving): Calories - 322; Fat - 2; Fiber - 9; Carbs - 63; Protein - 6

Delicious Risotto

(Prep + Cook Time: 30 minutes | Servings: 6)

Here's a simple way to prepare something that resembles Wolfgang Puck's famous perfect risotto. This works best with Arborio rice and Romano cheese.

Ingredients:

1 finely chopped medium onion
12 ounces Arborio rice
1 ½ tbsp olive oil
28 ounces chicken stock
3 tbsp Romano or Parmesan cheese
Salt and pepper to taste

Directions:

1. Heat the oil in the bottom of your cooker.
2. SAUTE the onion until soft and nearly translucent.
3. Add the rice and chicken stock.
4. Close the lid and select the RICE function. Set a timer for 15 minutes.
5. Wait for the cycle to end and for the pressure to naturally drop.
6. Open the lid and stir in a little bit of black pepper.
7. Add the Romano or Parmesan cheese.
8. Serve immediately.

Nutritional Info (per serving): Calories - 266; Fat – 4.8; Fiber – 1.7; Carbs – 46.3; Protein – 7.7

Mushroom and Pea Risotto

(Prep + Cook Time: 35 minutes | Servings: 4)

If you want to cook a unique risotto, you should use your Instant Pot. This recipe is easy to cook. You will be able to cook this nourishing and tasty Mushroom and Pea Risotto dish within half an hour.

Ingredients:

1 cup Arborio rice
2 tbsp butter (divided)
2 cups vegetable stock
½ cup onion (chopped)
1/8 cup white wine
1 cup mushrooms (sliced, sautéed)
½ cup peas (frozen)
½ tsp salt
Parmesan cheese (to taste)

Directions:

1. First of all, slice your mushrooms and place them in a frying pan. Add the butter, dried thyme, and salt. Start sautéing.
2. Cook for about 15 minutes till they are golden brown.
3. And then you should deglaze your skillet with the wine. Allow it to evaporate and then set it aside.
4. Set your Instant Pot to the SAUTE mode, and melt 1 tablespoon of butter.
5. After adding the chopped onions, keep sautéing for a couple of minutes.
6. Add the Arborio rice and keep stirring until transparent.
7. After deglazing your pan with the wine, you should add the vegetable stock, sautéed mushrooms, and salt. Stir the ingredients.
8. After covering the Instant Pot with the lid, you should press the MANUAL button and set the cooking time to 10 minutes at HIGH pressure.
9. Make sure that the pressure valve is set to the SEALING mode.
10. When the cooking time is over, you should do a quick pressure release by switching the pressure knob to the VENTING position.
11. Add 1/2 cup of frozen peas, the remaining butter and vegetable stock.
12. The peas will be ready in 3 minutes.
13. Cover them with the Parmesan cheese.

Butter Rice (S&F)

(Prep + Cook Time: 30 minutes | Servings: 4)

You will love this simple dish. This flavorful rice is creamy. To make it a complete meal, just mix in some caramelized onion and cooked mushrooms.

Ingredients:

1 ¼ cups beef stock

1 ¼ cups French Onion soup

1 stick (½ cup) butter

2 cups brown rice

Directions:

1. Put all of the ingredients in the Instant Pot. Stir to incorporate.
2. Close and lock the lid. Press MANUAL. Set to HIGH pressure and the time for 22 minutes.
3. When the timer beeps, let the pressure release naturally.
4. Serve warm. If desired, garnish with parsley.

Nutritional Info (per serving): Calories - 590; Fat – 26.3; Fiber – 3.8; Carbs – 78.7; Protein – 9.5

Vegetable Cajun Rice (VEG)

(Prep + Cook Time: 25 minutes | Servings: 4)

This flavorful dish is spicy and very satisfying. You can serve it as a main dish for two or as a side dish for four people. It's a simple dish filled with goodness.

Ingredients:

1 ½ heaped cups frozen vegetables
1 cup white basmati rice, washed in a sieve with cold running water
1 tsp olive oil
½ onion, finely diced
½ tsp ground cumin
½ tsp smoked paprika
1/3 tsp dried oregano
1/3 tsp dried thyme
¼- ½ tsp chili powder, less or more to taste
2 tbsp tomato purée, dissolve in
1 cup just boiled water

<u>Final seasoning</u>
1 tbsp fresh coriander, chopped
Salt and black pepper, to taste

Directions:
1. Press the SAUTE key of the Instant Pot.
2. Put the oil in the pot and add the onion; sauté until the edges of the onion is starting to brown and softened – this will add flavor to the dish.
3. Stir in the rice and add all the spices, stirring and mixing until well combined.
4. Add your preferred frozen veggies and the tomato puree dissolved in water.
5. Press the CANCEL key to stop the sauté function.
6. Cover and lock the lid. Press the MANUAL key, set the pressure to HIGH, and set the timer for 4 minutes.

7. When the Instant Pot timer beeps, press the CANCEL key.
8. Using an oven mitt or a long handled spoon, turn the steam valve to quick release the pressure.
9. Unlock and carefully open the lid. Using a fork, fluff the rice and then season well with black pepper and salt, 1 squeeze lime juice, and as much coriander as you desire.
10. You can leave out the coriander, but definitely season and squeeze with lime juice. Serve immediately.

Notes: Use small-sized frozen veggies in this dish, such as chopped onions and peppers, shelled soya beans or edamame, chopped green beans, sweet corn, and peas.

Nutritional Info (per serving): Calories - 471; Fat – 3.5; Fiber – 8.7; Carbs – 97.4; Protein – 11.4

Fried Rice

(Prep + Cook Time: 15 minutes | Servings: 4)

Fried rice in an instant pot? It's easy and the residual heat is just enough to warm your choice of veggies.

Ingredients:
1 tbsp butter (or oil)
1 medium onion, diced
2 cloves garlic, minced
1 egg
1 cup basmati rice, uncooked
¼ cup soy sauce
1 ½ cups chicken stock
½ cups peas, frozen OR your preferred vegetable

Directions:
1. Heat the instant pot to more SAUTE mode. Put the oil in the pot.
2. Add the garlic and the onion. Sauté for 1 minute.
3. Add the egg, scramble with the garlic mix for about 1-2 minutes.
4. Add the rice, stock, and soy sauce in the pot. Press CANCEL. Close and lock the lid. Press RICE and set the time for 10 minutes.
5. When the timer beeps, quick release the pressure. Carefully open the lid. Stir in the frozen peas or veggies.
6. Let sit until the peas/ veggies are warmed through.

Nutritional Info (per serving): Calories - 250; Fat – 4.6; Fiber – 2.3; Carbs – 44.2; Protein – 7.3

Cauliflower Rice (VEG)

(Prep + Cook Time: 25 minutes | Servings: 4)

Healthy cauliflower-rice is so easy to prepare with simple ingredients and taste delicious, without using a food processor or vegetable grater.

Ingredients:

1 medium-sized cauliflower head
2 tbsp olive oil
½ tsp salt
½ tsp dried parsley
¼ tsp ground cumin
¼ tsp turmeric powder
¼ tsp paprika
2 tbsp chopped cilantro
8 fluid oz water

Directions:

1. Remove and discard leaves from cauliflower, rinse and then cut into large pieces.
2. In the Instant Pot pour water, then insert a steamer basket and place cauliflower florets in it.
3. Plug in and switch on the Instant Pot, select steam option and secure pot with lid. Then position pressure indicator and adjust cooking time on timer pad to 1 minutes and let cook.
4. When the timer beeps, switch off the Instant Pot and do a quick pressure release.
5. Then uncover the pot and transfer cauliflower florets to a shallow dish.
6. Drain water in the pot, then switch on the Instant Pot and select SAUTE option and let heat.
7. Add oil, return cauliflower florets to the pot and mash using a potato masher.
8. Stir in all the spices until combined and cook until warm through.
9. Serve immediately.

Nutritional Info (per serving): Calories - 25; Fat – 0.1; Fiber – 2.5; Carbs – 5.3; Protein – 1.98

Bean Recipes

Steamed Green Beans

(Prep + Cook Time: 20 minutes | Servings: 4)

Cooking green beans in an Instant Pot is not only a time saver. It also preserves their color and nutrients.

Ingredients:

1 pound green beans, washed

1 cup water

2 tbsp fresh parsley, chopped, for garnish

For the dressing:

1 pinch ground black pepper

1 pinch salt

2 tbsp white wine vinegar

3 tbsp Parmesan cheese, freshly grated

3 tbsp olive oil

3 cloves garlic, sliced

Directions:

1. Pour the water into the Instant Pot and set the steamer basket. Put the green beans in the basket.
2. Press MANUAL, set the pressure to HIGH and the timer to 1 minute.
3. When the timer beeps, turn the valve to quick release the pressure.
4. Transfer the beans into a serving bowl.
5. Toss with the dressing Ingredients and let stand for 10 minutes. Remove the slices of garlic and then garnish with the parsley. Serve.

Nutritional Info (per serving): Calories - 143; Fat – 11.5; Fiber - 4; Carbs – 9.2; Protein – 3.5

Black Bean + Sweet Potato Hash (VEG)

(Prep + Cook Time: 15 minutes | Servings: 4)

Hashes make a great breakfast, because they're easy to make and easy to make nutritious. This one uses protein-heavy black beans and sweet potatoes. A little chili powder adds some heat to wake up even the sleepiest commuters.

Ingredients:

2 cups peeled, chopped sweet potatoes
1 cup chopped onion
1 cup cooked and drained black beans
1 minced garlic clove
⅓ cup veggie broth
¼ cup chopped scallions
2 tsp hot chili powder

Directions:

1. Prep your veggies.
2. Turn your Instant Pot to SAUTE and cook the chopped onion for 2-3 minutes, stirring so it doesn't burn.
3. Add the garlic and stir until fragrant. Add the sweet potatoes and chili powder, and stir.
4. Pour in the broth and give one last stir before locking the lid. Select MANUAL and cook on HIGH pressure for 3 minutes.
5. When time is up, quick-release the pressure carefully.
6. Add the black beans and scallions, and stir to heat everything up.
7. Season with salt and more chili powder if desired.

Nutritional Info (per serving): 133 Cal; 5 g protein; 28 g carbs; 9.5 g fiber.

White Bean Dip with Tomatoes (VEG)

(Prep + Cook Time: 15 minutes | Servings: 8)

This vegetarian dip is smoky and incredibly simple to make due to the basic ingredients used.

Ingredients:
1 can cannellini beans, soaked overnight
1 small white onion, peeled and diced
1 ½ tsp minced garlic, divided
6 sun-dried tomatoes
3 tbsp chopped parsley
1 tsp salt
1/8 tsp ground black pepper
1 tsp paprika
3 tbsp olive oil
2 tbsp lemon juice
1 tbsp capers

Directions:
1. Drain beans and place in the Instant Pot. Pour in water and add 1 teaspoon garlic, salt, and black pepper.
2. Plug in and switch on the Instant Pot and secure with lid. Then position pressure indicator, select MANUAL option and adjust cooking time on timer pad to 14 minutes and let cook.
3. When the timer beeps, switch off the Instant Pot and let pressure release naturally for 10 minutes and then do quick pressure release.
4. In the meantime, place a small non-stick frying pan over medium heat, add oil and let heat.
5. Then add onion and remaining garlic and cook for 3-5 minutes or until onions are nicely golden brown.
6. When the onions are done, set pan aside until required. Then uncover the pot and drain beans, reserve ½ cup of cooking liquid.
7. Let beans cool slightly and then transfer to a food processor and add onion-garlic mixture, paprika, and lemon juice.
8. Pulse until smooth, slowly blend in reserved cooking liquid until dip reaches to desired thickness. Tip mixture into a serving bowl.
9. Dice tomatoes and stir together with capers and parsley.
10. Add this mixture into bean dip and stir until mixed well.
11. Adjust the seasoning and serve immediately.

Nutritional Info (per serving): Calories - 47; Fat - 3; Fiber - 1; Carbs - 4; Protein - 2

Baked Beans

(Prep + Cook Time: 60 minutes | Servings: 8)

You can prepare a pound or more of baked beans with the following recipe. Serve with potato salad and coleslaw for a traditional Saturday supper. Remember to soak the beans the night before. This isn't always necessary when using a pressure cooker, but it can help soften the beans.

Ingredients:

½ a pound of bacon

2 small onions

2 cups navy beans (dried)

1 tsp dry mustard

½ tsp salt

4 ounces dark molasses

Directions:

1. Start by covering the beans with water in a bowl.
2. Soak the beans overnight. The next day, drain the water and rinse the beans. Remove any debris.
3. Place the beans in the pressure cooker.
4. Cover the beans with warm water. Don't fill more than halfway.
5. You should use LOW PRESSURE for 45 minutes.
6. Allow the pressure to drop naturally when the timer goes off. Carefully open the lid.
7. The beans should be soft and ready for consumption. If not, then continue cooking for a few more minutes.
8. Serve and enjoy!

Nutritional Info (per serving): Calories - 375; Fat – 13.7; Fiber - 13; Carbs – 49.2; Protein – 15.2

Beans Stew (VEG)

(Prep + Cook Time: 1 hour 25 minutes | Servings: 8)

It's a Colombian style beans stew. It's different, unique and very tasty.

Ingredients:
2 carrots, chopped
1 plantain, chopped
1 pound red beans, dry
Salt and black pepper to the taste
1 tomato, chopped
2 green onions stalks, chopped
1 small yellow onion, diced
¼ cup cilantro leaves, chopped
2 tbsp vegetable oil

Directions:
1. Put the beans in your Instant Pot, add water to cover, cook on HIGH pressure for 35 minutes and release pressure for 10 minutes naturally.
2. Add plantain, carrots, salt and pepper to the taste, cover Instant Pot again and cook on HIGH pressure for 30 more minutes.
3. Meanwhile, heat up a pan with the vegetable oil over medium high heat, add yellow onion, stir and cook for 2 minutes.
4. Add tomatoes, green onions, some salt and pepper, stir again, cook for 3 minutes more and take off the heat.
5. Release pressure naturally from your Instant Pot, divide cooked beans amongst plates, top with tomatoes and onions mix, sprinkle cilantro at the end and serve right away.
6. Serve.

Nutritional Info (per serving): 70 Cal; 3.1 g total fat; 9.6 g carbs; 1 g fiber; 3.6 g sugar; 2.5 g protein.

Stewed Tomatoes and Green Beans (VEG)

(Prep + Cook Time: 15 minutes | Servings: 6)

This simple and healthy side dish pairs tomatoes with green beans and garlic, resulting in bright and fresh flavors. You can use frozen green beans and canned tomatoes if you have to, though in my opinion, fresh is always better, if it's the season for it.

Ingredients:

1 pound trimmed green beans
2 cups fresh, chopped tomatoes
1 crushed garlic clove
1 tsp olive oil Salt

Directions:

1. Set SAUTE setting and preheat your Instant Pot.
2. When warm, add 1 teaspoon of olive oil and garlic.
3. When the garlic has become fragrant and golden, add tomatoes and stir. If the tomatoes are dry, add ½ cup water.
4. Fill the steamer basket with the green beans and sprinkle on salt. Lower into cooker.
5. Close and seal the lid. Select MANUAL and cook for 5 minutes on HIGH pressure.
6. When the timer beeps, turn off cooker and quick-release the pressure.
7. Carefully remove the steamer basket and pour beans into the tomato sauce.
8. If the beans aren't quite tender enough, simmer in sauce for a few minutes.
9. Serve.

Nutritional Info (per serving): Calories – 55.3; Fat – 3.2; Fiber – 2.6; Carbs – 6.3; Protein – 1.6

Three Bean Salad (VEG)

(Prep + Cook Time: 35 minutes | Servings: 4)

The vibrant colors and sweet and tart dressing makes this classic salad amazingly tasty and always a hit at parties.

Ingredients:

1 cup chickpeas, soaked for 30 minutes

1 cup cranberry beans, soaked for 30 minutes

1 ½ cups of green beans, fresh

2 celery stalks, chopped

Half of a medium red onion, peeled and chopped

1 tsp minced garlic

1 bay leaf

1 cup chopped parsley

1 tsp salt

½ tsp ground black pepper

1 tbsp coconut sugar

5 tbsp apple cider vinegar

4 tbsp olive oil

Directions:

1. Drain chickpeas and add to a 6-quarts Instant Pot. Pour in 4 cups water and then add garlic and bay leaf.
2. Insert a steamer basket and place placed drained cranberry beans in it.
3. Wrap French beans in an aluminum foil.
4. Place a small heatproof cup in the steamer basket and placed French beans packet on it.
5. Plug in and switch on the Instant Pot and secure pot with lid. Select MANUAL option and adjust cooking time on timer pad to 15 minutes and let cook.
6. In the meantime prepare the salad dressing. In a small bowl stir together onion, sugar, and vinegar and let macerate.

7. When the timer beeps, switch off the Instant Pot and let pressure release naturally for 10 minutes and then do quick pressure release.
8. Then uncover the pot, remove French beans packet and uncover.
9. Strain beans from steamer basket and Instant Pot, rinse under water until cool completely and then place in a large bowl.
10. Add French beans, prepared dressing, celery, parsley, olive oil, salt and black pepper and stir until well combined.
11. Chill salad before serving.

Nutritional Info (per serving): Calories - 200; Fat - 3; Fiber - 6; Carbs - 6; Protein - 4

Red Beans (VEG)

(Prep + Cook Time: 40 minutes | Servings: 8)

These beans are extremely flavorful and cooked with delicious Cajun ingredients like smoked sausage, onion, garlic, and celery. You can have the final product by itself as a side, or add cooked white rice for a complete protein.

Ingredients:

2 quarts water
1 pound rinsed red kidney beans (Overnight soaked)
1 tbsp salt 5 cups water
1 pound smoked sausage, cut into quarters lengthwise and then cut into ¼-inch pieces
4 sliced garlic cloves
2 bay leaves
1 big minced onion
1 seeded and minced green bell pepper
1 minced celery stalk
1 tsp olive oil
1 tsp dried thyme
1 tsp kosher salt
½ tsp salt
Black pepper

Directions:

1. The night before you plan on having the beans, go through them and throw out any bad ones.
2. Pour 2 quarts of water into a big bowl, add beans and salt, and soak overnight.
3. The next day, cook the aromatics. Pour 1 teaspoon oil into the pressure cooker and heat.
4. When shiny, add the celery, onion, pepper, thyme, garlic, sausage, and ½ teaspoon salt.

5. Stir while it's cooking, for 8 minutes, until the sausage and onions are starting to brown.
6. Drain and rinse off the beans.
7. Put them in the pressure cooker along with 1 teaspoon of salt and bay leaves.
8. Secure the lid and hit MANUAL. Select 15 minutes.
9. When time is up, hit CANCEL and wait 20 minutes. Open the cooker and pick out the bay leaves.
10. Take out 2 cups of the beans and liquid and blend until smooth.
11. Pour them back into the cooker.
12. You can simmer for another 15 minutes if you want, but it's not necessary. Serve!

Nutritional Info (per serving): Calories - 235; Fat - 17; Fiber - 14; Carbs - 11; Protein - 11

Chili Con Carne

(Prep + Cook Time: 30 minutes | Servings: 6)

You will definitely fall in love with this instant pot adaptation. It takes as little as 30 minutes, too!

Ingredients:

1 can (28 ounce) ground and peeled tomatoes
1 can (14 ounce) kidney beans, rinsed and drained
1 can (14 ounce) black beans, rinsed and drained
1 ½ pounds ground beef
1 ½ tsp ground cumin
1 ½ tsp salt
1 ½ cups onion, large diced
1 tbsp chili powder
1 tbsp Worcestershire Sauce
1 tsp dry oregano
½ cup fresh water
½ cup sweet red bell pepper, large dice
½ tsp freshly ground black pepper
1-2 jalapeños, medium-sized, stems and seeds removed, finely diced
2 tbsp garlic, minced
3 tbsp extra-virgin olive oil

Directions:

1. Press the SAUTE button. Let the instant pot heat. Put the oil in the pot.
2. Add the ground beef, sauté, breaking up using a wooden spoon, until the beef is slightly brown. Remove excess fat.
3. Add the onions, jalapenos, and bell pepper. Sauté for 3 minutes.
4. Add the garlic, chili powder, cumin, oregano, salt, and pepper. Sauté for 1 minute.
5. Add the beans, tomatoes, water, and Worcestershire sauce. Stir to combine. Close and lock the lid.
6. Set the pressure to HIGH and set the timer for 10 minutes.
7. When the timer beeps, let the pressure release for 10 minutes.
8. Turn the steam valve to release remaining pressure.
9. Serve immediately or simmer on less SAUTÉ for a thicker chili.

Nutritional Info (per serving): Calories - 772; Fat – 16.4; Fiber – 23.2; Carbs – 93.1; Protein – 65.7

Poultry Recipes

The Whole Chicken (S&F)

(Prep + Cook Time: 30 minutes | Servings: 8)

Want to make the easiest whole chicken in your pressure cooker? This recipe is so basic, it doesn't even need water. You can use any seasonings you want; the ingredients here are just suggestions.

Ingredients:

1 medium-sized, whole chicken

1 minced green onion

2 tbsp sugar

1 tbsp cooking wine

1 minced piece of ginger

2 tsp soy sauce

2 tsp salt

Directions:

1. Season the chicken thoroughly with salt and sugar.
2. Sprinkle 1 teaspoon of salt into the bottom of the Instant Pot.
3. Pour the wine and soy sauce into the cooker, and add the chicken.
4. Choose POULTRY and cook.
5. When time is up, flip the chicken, and push POULTRY again.
6. Let the pressure come down naturally before opening the cooker.
7. Serve chicken pieces with green onion on top and any side dishes you'd like.

Nutritional Info (per serving): Calories - 131; Fiber - 0; Carbs - 4; Protein - 18

Sticky Sesame Chicken (S&F)

(Prep + Cook Time: 30 minutes | Servings: 4)

You'll have to resist licking your fingers after enjoying this chicken dish. The chicken of choice is chicken thigh fillets, which stay more moist than chicken breasts, while the sauce is a mix of hoisin, sweet chili sauce, garlic, ginger, rice vinegar, and sesame seeds.

Ingredients:

6 boneless chicken thigh fillets

4 peeled and crushed garlic cloves

5 tbsp hoisin sauce

5 tbsp sweet chili sauce

½ cup chicken stock

1 chunk of peeled, grated fresh ginger

1 ½ tbsp sesame seeds

1 tbsp rice vinegar

1 tbsp soy sauce

Directions:

1. Spread chicken thighs flat and place them into the Instant Pot.
2. Whisk garlic, ginger, chili sauce, hoisin, vinegar, sesame seeds, broth, and soy sauce into a sauce.
3. Pour over chicken and stir.
4. Select MANUAL and then 15 minutes on HIGH pressure.
5. When time is up, hit CANCEL and wait for a natural pressure release.
6. When all the pressure is gone, open up the cooker and serve the chicken with rice.

Nutritional Info (per serving): Calories - 428; Fiber - 1; Carbs – 52.9; Protein - 30

Buttery Chicken

(Prep + Cook Time: 30 minutes | Servings: 4)

This dish is usually cooked in the slow cooker for 8 hours. With your Instant Pot, it will only take less than an hour.

Ingredients:

1 ½ pounds chicken thighs, skinless, cut into bite-sized pieces
1 can (15 ounce) tomato sauce
1 green bell pepper, chopped in large pieces
1 onion, diced
1 tsp coriander powder
1 tsp garam masala
1 tsp paprika
1 tsp salt
1 tsp turmeric
¼ tsp black pepper
¼ tsp cayenne
¼ tsp cumin
1-inch ginger, minced
2 tbs butter, grass-fed OR ghee, OR your choice of fat
5 garlic cloves, minced

After cooking:
1 cup coconut cream
Pinch dried fenugreek leaves (kasoori methi)
Cilantro, for garnish, optional

Directions:

1. Press the SAUTE key of the Instant Pot. Put the ghee and onion in the pot. Stir-fry the onion for about 8 to 10 minutes or until starting to brown.
2. Add the ginger and garlic; stir-fry for 30 seconds. Stir in the spices.

3. Add the chicken and mix well until combined. Continue stirring for about 4 to 5 minutes or until the chicken is seared.
4. Add the green bell pepper and tomato sauce. Cover and lock the lid. Turn the steam valve to SEALING.
5. Press the POULTRY key – this will automatically set the time for 15 minutes.
6. When the Instant Pot timer beeps, turn the steam valve to quick release the pressure or let the pressure release naturally. Unlock and carefully open the lid. Stir in the coconut cream and dried fenugreek leaves.
7. If desired, garnish with cilantro. Serve.

Nutritional Info (per serving): Calories - 507; Fat – 25.8; Fiber – 4.6; Carbs - 17; Protein – 53.3

Salsa Verde Chicken (S&F)

(Prep + Cook Time: 25 minutes | Servings: 6)

I love using salsa in recipes, because it's a cheap and easy way to add a ton of flavor to whatever dish it's in. In this case, it's salsa verde, and the dish is shredded chicken. You can use the finished product in a whole bunch of ways, like in a casserole, burrito, sandwich, taco, or over lettuce.

Ingredients:

2 ½ pounds of boneless chicken breasts

16 ounces of salsa verde

1 tsp smoked paprika

1 tsp cumin

1 tsp salt

Directions:

1. Throw everything into your Instant Pot pressure cooker.
2. Select MANUAL and then 25 minutes at HIGH pressure.
3. When the timer goes off, quick-release the pressure.
4. Carefully open the cooker and shred the chicken.
5. Serve and enjoy.

Nutritional Info (per serving): Calories - 340; Fat - 7; Fiber - 0; Carbs - 6; Protein - 59

Balsamic Chicken Thighs

(Prep + Cook Time: 25 minutes | Servings: 2)

Balsamic vinegar is one of the best marinades for just about anything, including chicken thighs. These balsamic-thighs are so easy, you just mix everything in a bag, cook some aromatics, and throw everything into the Instant Pot for just 15 minutes. It's a perfect weekday meal.

Ingredients:

1 pound boneless, skinless chicken thighs
½ cup balsamic vinegar
⅓ cup cream sherry wine
2 tbsp chopped cilantro
2 tbsp olive oil
2 tbsp minced green onion
1 ½ tsp minced garlic
1 tsp dried basil
1 tsp garlic powder
1 tsp Worcestershire sauce
½ tsp black pepper

Directions:

1. Mix basil, salt, garlic, pepper, sherry, Worcestershire, onion, and vinegar in a plastic bag.
2. Add chicken and squish around, so the chicken becomes completely coated. Turn your Instant Pot on and select SAUTE.
3. Pour in the olive oil and cook the minced garlic, stirring, until fragrant.
4. Turn the pot to POULTRY and pour in the chicken and sauce.
5. Secure the lid.
6. The POULTRY setting defaults to 15 minutes, which is the correct length of time for this recipe.
7. When it beeps, quick-release the pressure.
8. Serve with chopped cilantro and a side dish like rice or veggies.

Nutritional Info (per serving): Calories - 210; Fat - 12; Fiber - 0; Carbs - 10; Protein - 14

Italian Chicken

(Prep + Cook Time: 25 minutes | Servings: 6)

This particular Italian chicken is made with carrots, cremini mushrooms, cherry tomatoes, and green olives. If there's an ingredient a member of your family doesn't like, just leave it out.

Ingredients:

8 boneless, skinless chicken thighs
2 medium-sized, chopped carrots
½ pound stemmed and quartered cremini mushrooms
2 cups cherry tomatoes
3 smashed garlic cloves
½ cup pitted green olives
½ cup thinly-sliced fresh basil
¼ cup chopped fresh Italian parsley
1 chopped onion
1 tbsp olive oil
1 tbsp tomato paste
½ tsp black pepper
Salt to taste

Directions:

1. Season the chicken thighs with salt.
2. On your Instant Pot, hit SAUTE and pour in the olive oil.
3. When shiny, toss in the carrots, mushrooms, onions, and a little salt.
4. Cook for about 3-5 minutes until soft.
5. Add the smashed garlic and tomato paste and cook for another 30 seconds.
6. Last, add the cherry tomatoes, chicken thighs, and olives.
7. Turn off SAUTE before locking the pressure cooker.
8. Hit MANUAL and choose 10 minutes on HIGH Pressure
9. When the beeper goes off, quick-release the pressure right away.
10. Take off the lid and season. Serve.

Nutritional Info (per serving): Calories - 245; Fiber -3 ; Carbs - 10; Protein - 35

Chicken Noodle

(Prep + Cook Time: 30 minutes | Servings: 6)

Skip the instant noodles, which are packed with preservatives. This Instant Pot noodle recipe is easy and fast, and most of all, made with real food.

Ingredients:

For the soup:
2 pounds chicken thighs, boneless, skinless
1 package (1 pound) kelp noodles
1 piece (2 inches) ginger, peeled and grated
1 piece kombu
1 tbsp fish sauce, gluten-free
1 tbsp ghee (or, other cooking fat/ oil of your choice)
1/3 cup scallions, chopped
¼ tsp red pepper flakes
3 cloves garlic, large-sized, pressed
3 tbsp tamari (or coconut aminos)
6-8 cups chicken broth
Salt and pepper, to taste

For garnish:
Cilantro Extra scallions
Fresh squeezed lime juice

Directions:
1. Press the SAUTE key of the Instant Pot. Put the ghee in the pot and melt and heat.
2. When the ghee is hot, add the chicken thighs. Generously season with salt and pepper.
3. Add the ginger and garlic. Cook until all sides of the chicken thighs are browned, sealing the meat juices.
4. Add the broth, tamari, fish sauce, red pepper flakes, scallions, and kombu. Press the CANCEL key to stop the sauté function. Cover and lock the lid.

5. Press the MANUAL key, set the pressure to HIGH, and set the timer for 15 minutes.
6. When the Instant Pot timer beeps, turn the steam valve to quick release the pressure or let the pressure release naturally. Carefully open the lid and press the SAUTE key.
7. Remove the kombu pieces and set aside. You can use them again for another dish. With a pair of cooking tongs or with two forks, shred the chicken thighs.
8. Rinse the kelp noodles and then cut them to your desired length. Add into the pot. Stir to mix and let cook for a couple of minutes or until no longer crunchy and soft.
9. Divide between serving bowls. Garnish each serving with extra cilantro, scallion, and fresh squeezed lime juice.

Nutritional Info (per serving): Calories - 407; Fat – 9.8; Fiber – 1.4; Carbs – 22.8; Protein – 53.6

Hot Buffalo Wings

(Prep + Cook Time: 20 minutes | Servings: 6)

These hot wings are fabulous. They are made with only 7 ingredients and easy to prepare and make. Next time you are craving for mouth-watering wings, don't order out. Just make them yourself and save money.

Ingredients:

4 pounds chicken wing, sectioned, frozen or fresh
1-2 tbsp sugar, light brown
½ tsp kosher salt
½ cup cayenne pepper hot sauce (I used frank's red hot)
½ cup butter
1 tbsp Worcestershire sauce
6 ounces water

Directions:

For the sauce:
In a microwavable container, mix the hot sauce with the Worcestershire sauce, butter, salt, and brown sugar; microwave for 15 seconds or until the butter is melted.

For the wings:
1. Pour the water into the Instant Pot. Set a trivet in the bottom of the pot.
2. Put the chicken wings on the trivet. Cover and lock the lid. Press the MANUAL key, set the pressure to HIGH, and set the timer for 5 minutes.
3. When the Instant Pot timer beeps, release the pressure naturally for 5 minutes, then turn the steam valve to quick release the pressure.
4. Unlock and carefully open the lid. Put the oven rack in the center of the oven. Turn the oven to the broil.
5. Carefully transfer the chicken wings from the pot into a cookie sheet. Brush the tops of the chicken wings with the sauce.

6. Place the cookie sheet in the oven and broil for 5 minutes.
7. Turn the chicken wings and brush the other side with the remaining sauce.
8. Serve with celery sticks and blue cheese dressing.

Notes: If you want a hotter sauce, use more hot sauce. If you want a milder sauce, use more butter.

Nutritional Info (per serving): Calories - 603; Fat – 24.6; Fiber - 0; Carbs – 2.3; Protein – 87.9

Creamy Chicken and Mushroom

(Prep + Cook Time: 35 minutes | Servings: 4)

The secret of this creamy dish is the coconut cream. Coconut cream is different from coconut milk. It's what forms on top is when you chill coconut milk, separating from the coconut water.

Ingredients:

2 pounds chicken thighs

16 ounces baby portabella mushrooms, sliced

1 can coconut cream

Chicken broth, enough to fill the can of coconut cream after the coconut water is poured out

1 tsp dried thyme

1 tsp garlic powder

1 tsp onion powder

1 tsp salt

1 tbsp water

2 tbsp tapioca starch

Directions:
1. The night before cooking, chill the coconut cream can in the refrigerator overnight.
2. Before cooking, take the can out from the fridge and, without shaking the can, turn it upside down. Open the can. The coconut cream and water should be separated with the coconut water on top. Scoop or pour out the coconut water from the can.
3. Add chicken broth to replace the coconut water, filling the can to the top. Pour the broth and coconut cream into a medium-sized bowl.
4. Add the spices in the bowl. Whisk until well combined. Put the chicken in the Instant Pot.
5. Add the mushrooms on top of the chicken, covering the meat. Pour the coconut cream mix over the chicken and mushrooms. Cover and lock the lid. Press the MANUAL key, set the pressure to HIGH, and set the timer for 8 or 10 minutes.

6. When the Instant Pot timer beeps, let the pressure release naturally. Turn the steam valve to VENTING to release remaining pressure. Unlock and carefully open the lid.
7. With a slotted spoon, remove the mushroom and chicken from the pot, leaving the cooking liquid in the pot. Set aside the chicken and mushroom.
8. Discard ½ of the cooking liquid. Press the SAUTE key and bring to cooking liquid in the pot to a boil. In a small-sized bowl, combine the tapioca starch and water, whisking until smooth.
9. When the cooking liquid is boiling, whisk in the starch mixture until smooth and the liquid is thick as gravy. Turn off the Instant Pot.
10. Place the chicken and mushroom, ladle the gravy over, and serve.

Nutritional Info (per serving): Calories - 713; Fat – 41.1; Fiber – 3.5; Carbs – 14.8; Protein – 72.7

Chicken BBQ

(Prep + Cook Time: 30 minutes | Servings: 6)

This dish is comfort food at its quickest and at its best. The chicken, cooked first in an Instant Pot, comes out juicy and soft, instead of tough and dry. If you want a strong BBQ flavor, you can omit the cooking liquid and just brush the chicken directly with BBQ sauce before broiling.

Ingredients:

4-5 pound chicken thighs, bone-in or boneless, skinless, fat trimmed off
2 garlic cloves, chopped
1/8 tsp pepper, or more to taste
¼ tsp salt, or more to taste
½ cup PLUS 1 ½ tbsp water, divided
½ cup barbecue sauce (use your favorite)
1 tbsp olive oil
1 onion, medium-sized, chopped
1 ½ tbsp cornstarch

Directions:

1. Press the SAUTE key of the Instant Pot. Add the oil and heat.
2. Add the garlic and onion and sauté for about 1 to 2 minutes or until soft.
3. Stir in the 1/2 cup of water and barbecue sauce.
4. With the meaty side faced up, add the chicken in the pot. Press the CANCEL key to stop the sauté function. Cover and lock the lid.
5. Press the MANUAL key, set the pressure to HIGH, and set the timer for 10 minutes.
6. When the Instant Pot timer beeps, let the pressure release naturally. Turn the steam valve to release remaining pressure.
7. Unlock and carefully open the lid. Preheat the broiler. Grease a broiler pan and transfer the chicken into the greased pan.

8. Generously season both sides with salt and pepper. Arrange the chicken in the pan with the meaty side faced down. Set aside.
9. Press the SAUTE key of the Instant Pot. Bring the cooking liquid in pot to a boil. In a small-sized bowl, combine the cornstarch with 1 ½ tablespoon of water until smooth.
10. When the cooking liquid is boiling, add about ½ of the cornstarch mix into the pot, stir until the sauce is thick.
11. Add more cornstarch mix, if needed. Simmer the sauce until thick. Taste the sauce and, if needed, season with salt and pepper to taste.
12. Turn off the Instant Pot. Brush the top of the chicken with the sauce.
13. Place the pan 6 inches from the heat source and broil for about 2-3 minutes or until the chicken is glazed.
14. Remove the pan from the oven, flip the chicken, and brush the other side with the sauce.
15. Return the pan to the oven and broil for 2-3 minutes more or until the other side is glazed. Serve the chicken barbecue while it's still hot.
16. Serve the remaining sauce on the side.

Nutritional Info (per serving): Calories - 449; Fat – 9.9; Fiber – 0.5; Carbs – 9.8; Protein – 75.3

Honey-Sriracha Chicken

(Prep + Cook Time: 15 minutes | Servings: 4)

This is one of my favorite busy weekday meals. The sauce and chicken cook right in the Instant Pot together, as opposed to separate skillets, which is the usual method. The sauce can be spicy (3 tablespoons of sriracha) or sweeter with more honey. For having only 8 ingredients - including water - this is a meal rich in flavors.

Ingredients:

4 diced chicken breasts
¼ cup sugar
5 tbsp soy sauce
2-3 tbsp sriracha
2-3 tbsp honey
2 tbsp cornstarch
2 tbsp water + 2 tbsp cold water
1 tbsp minced garlic

Directions:

1. Mix soy sauce, honey, sriracha, sugar, 2 tablespoons of water, and garlic in your Instant Pot.
2. Add chicken and mix to coat in the sauce. Close and seal the lid. Select MANUAL and cook for 9 minutes on HIGH pressure.
3. When time is up, quick-release the pressure after turning the cooker off. In a cup, mix 2 tablespoons of cold water with cornstarch.
4. Turn the pot to SAUTE and pour in the cornstarch mixture.
5. Stir constantly until the pot boils and the sauce begins to thicken.
6. Serve over rice.

Nutritional Info (per serving): Calories - 419; Fat - 7; Carbs - 19; Protein - 67

Turkey Verde and Rice (S&F)

(Prep + Cook Time: 35 minutes | Servings: 4)

With just 5 ingredients, you have a healthy meal for dinner that is packed with bold flavor. It's very filling, thanks to wholesome brown rice and the turkey tenderloins that are cooked tender.

Ingredients:

2/3 cup chicken broth
1 ½ pounds turkey tenderloins (I used Jennie-O)
1 ¼ cup long grain brown rice
1 yellow onion, small-sized, sliced
½ cup salsa verde
½ tsp salt

Directions:

1. Put the rice in the Instant Pot. Pour in the broth.
2. Top the mix with the onion, turkey, and then the salsa. Sprinkle with the salt.
3. Cover and lock the lid. Press the MANUAL key, set the pressure to HIGH, and set the timer for 8 minutes.
4. When the Instant Pot timer beeps, let the pressure release naturally for 8 minutes. Turn the steam valve to release remaining pressure. Unlock and carefully open the lid.
5. Garnish each serving with fresh cilantro.

Nutritional Info (per serving): Calories - 421; Fat – 4.1; Fiber – 2.7; Carbs – 49.2; Protein – 48.1

Turkey Drumsticks

(Prep + Cook Time: 40 minutes | Servings: 5)

These turkey legs will remind you of the huge turkey legs you buy at state fairs or an amusement park. It only takes 7 ingredients to make and it's very easy, as well.

Ingredients:

6 turkey drumsticks

2 tsp brown sugar, packed tight

½ tsp garlic powder

½ cup water

½ cup soy sauce

1 tsp black pepper, fresh ground

1 tbsp kosher salt

Directions:

1. In a small-sized bowl, combine the garlic powder, pepper, brown sugar, and salt, breaking any clump of sugar.
2. Season the turkey drumsticks with the seasoning mix. Pour the water in the Instant Pot. Add the soy sauce.
3. Add the seasoned drumsticks with any remaining seasoning mix.
4. Cover and lock the lid. Press the MANUAL key, set the pressure to HIGH, and set the timer for 25 minutes.
5. When the Instant Pot timer beeps, let the pressure release naturally for 15 minutes. Turn the steam valve to release remaining pressure. Unlock and carefully open the lid.
6. Using tongs, carefully transfer the drumsticks into a serving plate – be very careful because the drumsticks are cooked to fall-off-the-bone tender.
7. If you have time, pour the cooking liquid into a fat strainer. Let the fat float to the top.
8. Pass the defatted cooking liquid at the table as a sauce.

Nutritional Info (per serving): Calories - 209; Fat - 0; Fiber - 0; Carbs - 3; Protein – 34.6

Stuffed Turkey Tenderloin

(Prep + Cook Time: 30 minutes | Servings: 6)

With an Instant Pot in the kitchen, you can make Thanksgiving dishes all year-round. When this dish is cooked, your kitchen will smell as if you spent hours preparing it – just don't let them know it took only half an hour.

Ingredients:

2 turkey breast tenderloins

2 cups white rice

2 bacon slices, diced

1-2 sprigs fresh rosemary, optional

½ cup dry white wine

1 tsp fresh rosemary, chopped

1 cup fresh cranberries

1 ½ cups butternut squash, diced, frozen or fresh

3 ½ cups chicken broth OR water

Directions:

1. Press the SAUTE key of the Instant Pot.
2. Add the bacon in the pot and sauté until some of the fat rendered and the edges start to crisp.
3. Add the squash and cranberries, along with the rosemary. Sauté until the edges of the squash are golden and the bacon is crisp. Turn the Instant Pot off.
4. Butterfly the turkey tenderloins by slicing them gently lengthwise, going almost all the way through the other edge, making sure to leave the other edge intact. Open the tenderloins like a butterfly.
5. When the butternut mix is cooked, gently spoon the mix into the center of each butterflied turkey. Fold the tenderloin back.
6. Weave a rosemary sprig through the open edge of the tenderloin to seal. Alternatively, you can use a cooking twine. Press the SAUTÉ key of the Instant Pot.
7. When the pot is hot, cook the tenderloins for about 3 to 4 minutes per side or until both sides are golden.

8. Remove the browned tenderloins from the pot.
9. Add the rice in the pot and sauté for about 1 to 2 minutes or just until the rice begins to smell nutty.
10. Add the white wine in the pot to deglaze, stirring and scraping the browned bits off the bottom using a wooden spoon.
11. Add the broth and water in the pot. Place the stuffed tenderloin on top of the rice.
12. If desired, add the rosemary sprigs in the pot. Cover and lock the lid. Press the RICE key.
13. When the Instant Pot timer beeps, release the pressure naturally for 10 minutes.
14. Turn the steam valve to VENTING to release remaining pressure. Unlock and carefully open the lid. Remove the rosemary sprigs and then slice the tenderloin. Serve.

Nutritional Info (per serving): Calories - 447; Fat – 5.5; Fiber – 2.5; Carbs – 56.7; Protein – 38.1

Thanksgiving Turkey Casserole

(Prep + Cook Time: 45 minutes | Servings: 4)

This dish is delicious that there won't be any leftovers if you make it for a family of four or when you have guests over. This recipe pairs well with garlic and rosemary mashed potatoes.

Ingredients:

4 turkey breasts, boneless (about 2 pounds), or chicken breasts
2 small-sized cans cream of mushroom soup
1 stalk celery
1 onion, sliced
1 cup chicken broth
1 bag Pepperidge farms stuffing cubes
1 bag frozen mixed veggies

Directions:

1. Put the turkey breasts in the Instant Pot.
2. Add the broth, mixed vegetables, celery, and onion. Cover and lock the lid. Press the MANUAL key, set the pressure to HIGH, and set the timer for 25 minutes. Alternatively, you can press the POULTRY setting and adjust the timer for 25 minutes.
3. When the Instant Pot timer beeps, turn the steam valve to quick release the pressure. Unlock and carefully open the lid.
4. Add the stuffing cubes in the pot on top of the cooked mix. Pour in the cream of mushroom soup.
5. Press the SAUTE key and cook for 8 minutes.
6. Press CANCEL to stop the sauté function. Shred the turkey breast right in the pot. Serve.

Nutritional Info (per serving): Calories - 650; Fat – 20.1; Fiber – 7.2; Carbs – 66.5; Protein – 48.7

Egg Recipes

Hard-Boiled Eggs (S&F)

(Prep + Cook Time: 9 minutes | Servings: 6)

Ingredients:

12 large white eggs

1 cup of water

Directions:
1. In the Instant Pot Pour down about 1 cup of water into the bowl.
2. Place stainless steamer basket inside the pot.
3. Place the eggs in the steamer basket.
4. Boil 7 minutes on manual HIGH pressure
5. Then release the pressure through the quick release valve.
6. Open up the lid and take out the eggs using tongs and dunk them into a bowl of cold water.

Soft-Boiled Egg (S&F)

(Prep + Cook Time: 6 minutes | Servings: 2)

Ingredients:

4 eggs

1 cup of water

Two toasted English muffins

Salt and pepper to taste

Directions:

1. Pour 1 cup of water into the Instant Pot and insert the steamer basket. Put four canning lids into the basket before placing the eggs on top of them, so they stay separated.
2. Secure the lid.
3. Press the STEAM setting and choose 4 minutes.
4. When ready, quick-release the steam valve.
5. Take out the eggs using tongs and dunk them into a bowl of cold water.
6. Wait 1-2 minutes.
7. Peel and serve with one egg per half of a toasted English muffin.
8. Season with salt and pepper.

Delightful Soft Eggs

(Prep + Cook Time: 10 minutes | Servings: 4)

This delightful dish can be your favorite kind of the breakfast. Try it once and you will love it forever!

Ingredients:

3 eggs

6 oz ham

1 tsp salt

½ tsp ground white pepper

1 tsp paprika

¼ tsp ground ginger

2 tbsp chives

Directions:
1. Take the small ramekins and beat the eggs in them.
2. Sprinkle the eggs with the salt, ground black pepper, and paprika.
3. Transfer the ramekins to the Instant Pot and set the mode STEAM. Close the lid and cook the dish for 4 minutes.
4. Meanwhile, chop the ham and chives and combine the ingredients together.
5. Add ground ginger and stir the mixture carefully.
6. Transfer the mixture to the serving plates.
7. When the time is over – remove the eggs from the Instant Pot and put them over the ham mixture.
8. Serve the dish immediately. Enjoy!

Nutritional Info (per serving): Calories - 205; Fat – 11.1; Fiber - 1; Carbs – 6.47; Protein - 19

French Toast Bake

(Prep + Cook Time: 35 minutes | Servings: 4)

You don't have to go out for breakfast to get really good French toast. A dish that's notorious to get just right is made easy in the Instant Pot, and you'll want to make it again and again. Buy some cinnamon-raisin bread, let it go stale, and you'll be ready to make a delicious French-toast bake the whole family will love.

Ingredients:

3 big, beaten eggs
3 cups stale cinnamon-raisin bread, cut into cubes
1 ½ cups water
1 cup whole milk
2 tbsp maple syrup
1 tsp butter
1 tsp sugar
1 tsp pure vanilla extract

Directions:

1. Pour the water into your Instant Pot and lower in the steam rack.
2. Grease a 6-7 inch soufflé pan.
3. In a bowl, mix milk, vanilla, maple syrup, and eggs.
4. Add the bread cubes and let them soak for 5 minutes.
5. Pour into the pan, making sure the bread is totally submerged.
6. Set in the pressure cooker.
7. Hit MANUAL and adjust the time to 15 minutes on HIGH pressure
8. Quick-release the pressure when time is up.
9. Sprinkle the top with sugar and broil in the oven for 3 minutes.

Nutritional Info (per serving): Calories - 183; Fat - 3; Fiber - 3; Carbs - 21; Protein - 8

Poached Tomato Eggs

(Prep + Cook Time: 15 minutes | Servings: 4)

It is better to use the fresh tomatoes for the dish – it will make it juicy and aromatic.

Ingredients:

4 eggs

3 medium tomatoes

1 red onion

1 tsp salt

1 tbsp olive oil

½ tsp white pepper

½ tsp paprika

1 tbsp fresh dill

Directions:
1. Spray the ramekins with the olive oil inside.
2. Beat the eggs in every ramekin.
3. Combine the paprika, white pepper, fresh dill, and salt together in the mixing bowl. Stir the mixture.
4. After this, chop the red onion.
5. Chop the tomatoes into the tiny pieces and combine them with the onion. Stir the mixture.
6. Then sprinkle the eggs with the tomato mixture.
7. Add spice mixture and transfer the eggs to the Instant Pot.
8. Close the lid and set the Instant Pot mode STEAM.
9. Cook the dish for 5 minutes. Then remove the dish from the Instant Pot and chill it little.
10. Serve the dish immediately. Enjoy!

Nutritional Info (per serving): Calories - 194; Fat – 13.5; Fiber - 2; Carbs - 10; Protein - 10

Scrambled Eggs (S&F)

(Prep + Cook Time: 15 minutes | Servings: 4)

The scrambled eggs are very delightful and tender. It is the nutritious dish for breakfast.

Ingredients:

7 eggs

½ cup milk

1 tbsp butter

1 tsp basil

¼ cup fresh parsley

1 tsp salt

1 tsp paprika

4 oz bacon

1 tbsp cilantro

Directions:
1. Beat the eggs in the mixing bowl and whisk them well.
2. Then add milk, basil, salt, paprika, and cilantro. Stir the mixture. Chop the bacon and parsley.
3. Set the Instant Pot mode SAUTE and transfer the chopped bacon. Cook it for 3 minutes.
4. Then add whisked egg mixture and cook the dish for 5 minutes more.
5. After this, mix up the eggs carefully with the help of the wooden spoon.
6. Then sprinkle the dish with the chopped parsley and cook it for 4 minutes more.
7. When the eggs are cooked – remove them from the Instant Pot.
8. Serve the dish immediately. Enjoy!

Nutritional Info (per serving): Calories - 290; Fat – 23.4; Fiber - 1; Carbs – 4.53; Protein - 16

Aromatic Bacon Eggs

(Prep + Cook Time: 15 minutes | Servings: 4)

This dish is very delightful and should be served only hot.

Ingredients:
7 oz bacon
4 eggs, boiled
1 tsp cilantro
½ cup spinach
2 tsp butter
½ tsp ground white pepper
3 tbsp cream

Directions:
1. Slice the bacon and sprinkle it with the ground white pepper, and cilantro. Stir the mixture.
2. Peel eggs and wrap them in the spinach leaves.
3. Then wrap the eggs in the sliced bacon.
4. Set the Instant Pot mode MEAT/STEW and transfer the wrapped eggs.
5. Add butter and cook the dish for 10 minutes.
6. When the time is over – remove the eggs from the Instant Pot and sprinkle them with the cream.
7. Serve the dish hot.

Nutritional Info (per serving): Calories - 325; Fat – 28.4; Fiber - 2; Carbs – 5.24; Protein - 15

Cheesy Sausage Frittata

(Prep + Cook Time: 45 minutes | Servings: 4)

Cooked on low pressure, eggs and sausage blend with cheese for a hearty, hot breakfast that will leave you ready to take on whatever kind of day you have ahead of you. Frittatas are flexible, so you can add bacon and onion if you'd like.

Ingredients:

1 ½ cups water

4 beaten eggs

½ cup cooked ground sausage

¼ cup grated sharp cheddar

2 tbsp sour cream

1 tbsp butter

Salt to taste

Black pepper to taste

Directions:

1. Pour water into the Instant Pot and lower in the steamer rack.
2. Grease a 6-7 inch soufflé dish.
3. In a bowl, whisk the eggs and sour cream together.
4. Add cheese, sausage, salt, and pepper. Stir.
5. Pour into the dish and wrap tightly with foil all over.
6. Lower into the steam rack and close the pot lid.
7. Hit MANUAL and then 17 minutes on LOW pressure.
8. Quick-release the pressure. Serve hot!

Nutritional Info (per serving): Calories - 282; Fat - 12; Fiber - 12; Carbs - 1; Protein - 16

Savory Breakfast Egg Porridge

(Prep + Cook Time: 60 minutes | Servings: 4)

A lot of breakfast foods, especially porridge, are sweet. If you're a person who frequently eats leftovers for breakfast, this rice porridge with scallions, soy sauce, and egg will satisfy that savory tooth.

Ingredients:

2 cups chicken broth

2 cups water

4 eggs

4 chopped scallions

½ cup rinsed and drained white rice

1 tbsp sugar

1 tbsp olive oil

2 tsp soy sauce

½ tsp salt Black pepper

Directions:

1. Pour water, broth, sugar, salt, and rice into the Instant Pot. Close the lid.
2. Hit PORRIDGE and 30 minutes on HIGH pressure.
3. While that cooks, heat oil in a saucepan.
4. Crack in the eggs one at a time, so they aren't touching each other.
5. Cook until the whites become crispy on the edges, but the yolks are still runny. Sprinkle on salt and pepper.
6. When the Instant Pot timer goes off, hit CANCEL and wait for the pressure to go down on its own.
7. If the porridge isn't thick enough, hit SAUTE and cook uncovered for 5-10 minutes.
8. Serve with scallions, soy sauce, and an egg per bowl.

Nutritional Info (per serving): Calories - 214; Fat - 2; Fiber - 2; Carbs - 24; Protein - 10

Beef Recipes

Marinated Steak

(Prep + Cook Time: 45 minutes | Servings: 4)

This steakhouse flavored meat is a fantastic meal straight from your Instant Pot. It's simple and only requires 4 ingredients to make. Each serving is very low in sugar and high in niacin, selenium, and zinc.

Ingredients:

2 pounds flank steak
2 tbsp onion soup mix, dried
¼ cups apple cider vinegar
½ cups olive oil
1 tbsp Worcestershire sauce

Directions:

1. Press the SAUTE key of the Instant Pot.
2. Put the flank steak in the pot and cook each side until browned.
3. Add the Worcestershire sauce, vinegar, onion soup mix, and olive oil.
4. Press the CANCEL key to stop the sauté function. Cover and lock the lid.
5. Press the MEAT/ STEW key, set the pressure to HIGH, and set the timer for 35 minutes.
6. When the Instant Pot timer beeps, turn the steam valve to quick release the pressure.
7. Unlock and carefully open the lid. Serve!

Nutritional Info (per serving): Calories - 684; Fat – 44.1; Fiber - 0; Carbs – 5.5; Protein – 63.6

Beef Stroganoff

(Prep + Cook Time: 10 minutes | Servings: 4)

This filling, hearty dish is a great meal after a tiring day. Each serving is low in sugar, high in selenium, and very high in vitamin B6.

Ingredients:

1 pound steak, thin-cut

1 cup sour cream

1 onion, small-sized

16 ounces egg noodles

4 cups beef broth

4 tbsp butter

8 ounces mushrooms, sliced

Directions:

1. Dice the onion into small-sized pieces. Cut the steak into thin pieces. Press the SAUTÉ key of the Instant Pot.
2. Add the butter, onion, and steak and wait until the butter is melted.
3. Add the mushrooms, broth, and egg noodle.
4. Press the CANCEL key to stop the sauté function. Cover and lock the lid. Press the MANUAL key, set the pressure to HIGH, and set the timer for 4 minutes.
5. When the Instant Pot timer beeps, turn the steam valve to quick release the pressure. Unlock and carefully open the lid.
6. Stir in the sour cream and serve.

Nutritional Info (per serving): Calories - 669; Fat – 33.1; Fiber – 2.5; Carbs – 36.3; Protein - 55

Garlic Teriyaki Beef

(Prep + Cook Time: 55 minutes | Servings: 4)

This teriyaki recipe is made using cheaper cut beef, which is perfectly okay because the Instant Pot cooks it to deliciously tender pieces. This silky, sweet dish will definitely fix your craving for Chinese flavor.

Ingredients:

1 piece (2 pounds) flank steak
2 cloves garlic, finely chopped
For the teriyaki sauce:
2 tbsp fish sauce
¼ cup maple syrup, preferably organic grade B or higher
¼ cup coconut aminos OR soy sauce instead
1 tbsp raw honey
1 ½ tsp ground or fresh ginger, optional

Directions:

1. Slice the flank steak into 1/2-inch strips.
2. In a bowl, put all of the teriyaki sauce and mix until combined.
3. Put the steak strips and the sauce in the Instant Pot – there is no need to brown the meat. Cover and lock the lid.
4. Press the MANUAL key, set the pressure to HIGH, and set the timer for 40 minutes.

Nutritional Info (per serving): Calories - 351; Fat – 12.7; Fiber - 0; Carbs – 13.2; Protein – 43.7

Beef And Broccoli

(Prep + Cook Time: 50 minutes | Servings: 4)

This Instant Pot recipe is a copycat of a Chinese takeout. Each serving is very high in iron, vitamin B6, vitamin B12, vitamin C, and selenium, and high in niacin, phosphorus, and zinc. Serve with rice or cauliflower rice.

Ingredients:

1 pound stew beef meat, grass fed
1 bag (10-12 ounces) frozen broccoli, preferably organic
1 clove garlic, large-sized, pressed
1 onion, quartered
1 tsp ground ginger
½ cup beef or bone broth
½ tsp salt
¼ cup coconut aminos
2 tbsp fish sauce

Directions:

1. Except for the broccoli, put the rest of the ingredients in the Instant Pot. Cover and lock the lid.
2. Press the MEAT/ STEW key, and cook on pre-set time.
3. When the Instant Pot timer beeps, press the OFF key and turn the steam valve to quick release the pressure. Unlock and carefully open the lid.
4. Add the broccoli, loosely cover with the lid, and let sit for 15 minutes. Serve!

Nutritional Info (per serving): Calories - 267; Fat – 7.5; Fiber – 2.7; Carbs – 9.3; Protein – 39.7

Italian Beef

(Prep + Cook Time: 40 minutes | Servings: 6)

This perfectly seasoned Instant Pot version is a hearty meal. The beef comes out fall-apart-fork-tender. It's perfect with your favorite creamy mashed potato recipe or any vegetable you prefer.

Ingredients:

3 ½ pounds beef roast
16 ounces whole tomatoes, canned
2 whole bay leaves
2 tsp bouillon, beef, granules
¼ tsp black pepper
¼ cups water
½ tsp pickling spice
½ tsp garlic, minced, #1
1 tsp salt
1 tbsp wine vinegar
3 cloves garlic, medium-sized #2

Directions:

1. Trim the fat off the beef and cut to fit inside the inner pot.
2. Put the rest of the ingredients in the pot, placing them over the beef. Cover and lock the lid.
3. Press the MEAT/ STEW key, set the pressure to HIGH, and set the timer for 35 minutes.
4. When the Instant Pot timer beeps, turn the steam valve to quick release the pressure. Unlock and carefully open the lid.
5. Remove the bay leaf and serve.

Nutritional Info (per serving): Calories - 515; Fat – 16.8; Fiber – 1.4; Carbs – 7.6; Protein – 81.4

Korean Beef

(Prep + Cook Time: 75 minutes | Servings: 6)

This flavorful dish is amazing. Serve over rice or cauliflower rice. You can also make Korean beef tacos.

Ingredients:
4 pounds bottom roast, cut into cubes
1 apple, Granny Smith or pear, peeled and then chopped
2 tbsp olive oil
½ cup soy sauce
1 tbsp ginger, fresh grated
1 large orange OR
2 small orange, juice only
1 cup beef broth
5 cloves garlic, minced
Salt and pepper

Directions:
1. Season the roast cubes generously with pepper and salt. Press the SAUTE key of the instant pot.
2. When the pot is hot, coat with the olive oil. In batches, cook the meat until all sides are browned –transfer the browned meat into a plate while cooking.
3. When all the meat is browned, pour the beef broth in the pot and deglaze the pot – scrape the browned bits off from the bottom of the pot.
4. Pour the soy sauce in the pot and stir to mix. Return all the browned meat into the pot.
5. Add the ginger, garlic, and pear /apple on top of the meat. Lightly stir to combine slightly.
6. Add the orange juice.
7. Press the CANCEL key to stop the sauté function. Cover and lock the lid. Press the MANUAL key, set the pressure to HIGH, and set the timer for 45 minutes.
8. When the instant pot timer beeps, turn the steam valve to VENTING to quick release the pressure. Unlock and carefully open the lid.
9. Serve over rice or cauliflower rice.

Nutritional Info (per serving): Calories - 654; Fat – 23.9; Fiber – 1.8; Carbs – 10.4; Protein – 94.5

Beef Short Ribs

(Prep + Cook Time: 60 minutes | Servings: 6)

This dish is usually a weekend treat, but with an Instant Pot, you can cook it even during busy weeknights. This meal comes out fast and hearty.

Ingredients:
4 pounds beef short ribs
4-6 carrots, cut into bite sized pieces
3 cloves garlic, minced
2 tbsp olive oil
2 cups onions, diced
1 tbsp dried thyme
1 ½ cups beef broth
Kosher salt and fresh cracked pepper

Directions:
1. Press the SAUTE key of the Instant Pot. Pat dry the short ribs and generously season with the pepper and salt.
2. Drizzle olive oil in the pot and, in one single layer at a time, put the ribs in the pot and cook for about 4-5 minutes each side or until all the sides are browned – do not crowd the pot, so brown the short ribs in batches.
3. Transfer the browned short ribs into a plate and set aside.
4. Put the garlic in the pot and sauté, constantly stirring, for about 1 minute. Add the onion, carrot, and thyme. Season to taste with more salt and pepper.
5. Cook for about 4 to 5, occasionally stirring, until the veggies are soft. Return the browned short ribs into the pot. Press the CANCEL key to stop the sauté function. Cover and lock the lid.
6. Press the MANUAL key, set the pressure to HIGH, and set the timer for 35 minutes.
7. When the Instant Pot timer beeps, release the pressure naturally for 10-15 minutes or until the valve drops.
8. Turn the steam valve to release remaining pressure.
9. Unlock and carefully open the lid. Serve hot.

Nutritional Info (per serving): Calories - 705; Fat – 32.3; Fiber - 2; Carbs – 8.6; Protein – 89.4

Beefy Lasagna

(Prep + Cook Time: 40 minutes | Servings: 6)

This is lasagna as you know and love it - lots of beef, cheese, and delicious ricotta filling. You don't even have to boil the noodles beforehand, just get the oven-ready no-boil variety. With an Instant Pot, lasagna becomes a 30-minute meal!

Ingredients:

2 pounds ricotta cheese

1 pound of ground beef

24-ounces pasta sauce

8-ounces of no-boil lasagna noodles

1 package shredded mozzarella cheese

2 big eggs

¼ cup water

⅓ cup grated Parmesan

1 diced onion

1 tbsp olive oil

2 tsp minced garlic

1 tsp Italian seasoning

Salt and pepper to taste

Directions:
1. Pour olive oil in your Instant Pot and heat until it starts to smoke.
2. Quickly add the ground beef, onions, salt, and pepper.
3. When the meat is brown and onions clear, pour in the water and pasta sauce.
4. Stir before pouring out into a bowl.
5. In a separate bowl, mix the ricotta, garlic, Italian seasoning, eggs, Parmesan, salt, and pepper together.
6. Fill the pressure cooker with ¼ inch of water.
7. Layer ⅙ of the beef mixture into the bottom before adding the noodles.
8. Pour in ⅓ of the ricotta mixture, and then more beef sauce.

9. Top with noodles, and keep going until you've used everything. The last layer should be beef sauce.
10. Close the Instant Pot lid.
11. Select MANUAL, and then 7 minutes on HIGH pressure.
12. When the beep sounds, press CANCEL and quick-release the pressure.
13. Open the lid and sprinkle on the mozzarella.
14. Cool for a few minutes before serving.

Nutritional Info (per serving): Calories - 408; Fat – 22.1; Fiber – 2.6; Carbs – 27.4; Protein – 25.1

Balsamic Maple Beef

(Prep + Cook Time: 55 minutes | Servings: 6)

Each serving of this dish is high in selenium and vitamin B12 and very high in zinc. It's a simple dish that only takes a couple of ingredients to make –most f them you probably have on-hand.

Ingredients:
3 pounds chuck steak, boneless, fat trimmed, sliced into ½-inch strips
2 tbsp avocado oil OR olive oil
½ cup balsamic vinegar
1 tsp ground ginger
1 tsp garlic, finely chopped
1 cup maple syrup
1 cup bone broth
1 ½ tsp salt

Directions:
1. Trim the fat off from the joint the beef and slice the meat into 1/2-inch thin strips. In a bowl, mix the ground ginger with the salt. Season the meat with the ginger mix.
2. Press the SAUTE key of the Instant Pot. Put the oil in the pot and heat.
3. When the oil is hot and shimmery, but not smoking, add the beef and cook until all sides are browned – you will have to cook in batches.
4. Transfer the browned beef into a plate and set aside. Put the garlic in the pot and sauté for about 1 minute.
5. Add the broth, maple syrup, and balsamic vinegar. Stir to mix. Return the browned beef into the pot.
6. Press the CANCEL key to stop the sauté function. Cover and lock the lid.
7. Press the MANUAL key, set the pressure to HIGH, and set the timer for 35 minutes.
8. When the Instant Pot timer beeps, turn the steam valve to VENTING to quick release the pressure.
9. Unlock and carefully open the lid. If desired, you can thicken the sauce. Press the SAUTE key.
10. Mix 4 tablespoons arrowroot or tapioca starch with 4 tablespoons water until smooth and then add into the pot; cook for about 5 minutes or until the sauce is thick. Serve!

Nutritional Info (per serving): Calories - 721; Fat – 30.5; Fiber - 0; Carbs – 36.1; Protein - 71

Mississippi Pot Roast

(Prep + Cook Time: 55 minutes | Servings: 6)

This delicious beef dish is as simple as it gets. Each serving is low in sugar, high in phosphorus, vitamin A, and zinc, and very high in iron, selenium, vitamin B6, vitamin B12, and vitamin C.

Ingredients:

5-6 pounds beef, arm or chuck roast
½ cup beef broth
½ cup pepperoncini juice
1 envelope ranch dressing mix
1 envelope au jus gravy mix (or brown gravy mix)
¼ cup butter
6-8 pepperoncini

Directions:

1. Pour the pepperoncini juice and the broth in the pot.
2. Add the roast beef. Sprinkle the gravy and the dressing mix over the roast, and then top with the butter and pepperoncini. Cover and lock the lid.
3. Press the MANUAL key, set the pressure to HIGH, and set the timer for 90 minutes.
4. When the Instant Pot timer beeps, turn off the pot, release the pressure naturally for 10-15 minutes or until the valve drops.
5. Turn the steam valve to release remaining pressure.
6. Unlock and carefully open the lid.

Nutritional Info (per serving): Calories - 828; Fat - 32; Fiber – 1.7; Carbs – 11.4; Protein – 116.9

Instant Pot Roast

(Prep + Cook Time: 55 minutes | Servings: 8)

This pot roast supper is enough to serve 8, which makes it a great option for a dinner party where you want to serve something easy, hearty, and satisfying.

Ingredients:

4 pounds bottom roast cut into cubes
1 cup beef broth
5 minced garlic cloves
1 peeled and chopped Granny Smith apple
1 thumb of grated ginger
½ cup soy sauce
Juice of one big orange
2 tbsp olive oil
Salt and pepper to taste

Directions:
1. Season the roast with salt and pepper. Turn on your Instant Pot to SAUTE.
2. When hot, pour in the olive oil and brown the roast all over.
3. Move the meat to a plate.
4. Pour in the beef broth and scrape any stuck bits of meat.
5. Pour in soy sauce and stir.
6. Put the roast back into the pot.
7. Arrange the cut apple, garlic, and ginger on top.
8. Pour in the orange juice. Close the pressure cooker lid.
9. Select MANUAL and then 45 minutes on HIGH pressure.
10. Hit CANCEL and quick-release the pressure when the timer beeps. Serve!

Nutritional Info (per serving): 492 Cal; 46 g protein; 3 g carbs; 0 g fiber; 37 g fat.

Teriyaki Short Ribs

(Prep + Cook Time: 45 minutes | Servings: 4)

These lip-smacking beef short ribs are packed with umami flavor from ginger, brown sugar, soy sauce, orange, and sesame oil. The beef is marinated for at least 4 hours, though you can go a full 24 for a really full flavor. You can serve with rice or a favorite veggie as a side.

Ingredients:

4 big beef short ribs
1 cup water
¾ cup soy sauce
1 big, halved orange
½ cup brown sugar
1 full garlic bulb, peeled and crushed
1 large thumb of peeled and crushed fresh ginger
½ tbsp sesame oil
Dried pepper flakes
A bunch of chopped green onions

Directions:

1. In a Ziploc bag, mix water, sugar, and soy sauce.
2. Squish around until the sugar has dissolved.
3. Add the orange juice and stir, before adding the orange slices as well.
4. Lastly, throw in the garlic, ginger, onions, and dried pepper flakes.
5. Stir before adding the ribs.
6. Stir one last time and marinate in the fridge for at least 4 hours.
7. When ready to cook the ribs, coat the bottom of the Instant Pot with olive oil and heat.
8. Remove the ribs from the bag (save the liquid!) with tongs and quickly sear for 2-3 minutes on both sides.
9. Pour in the marinade and close the lid.
10. Select the MEAT/STEW setting and select 30 minutes.
11. When time is up, press CANCEL and quick-release the pressure. Serve!

Nutritional Info (per serving): Calories - 603; Fat - 10; Fiber - 1; Carbs - 76; Protein - 43

Sweet-Spicy Meatloaf

(Prep + Cook Time: 55 minutes | Servings: 4)

Meatloaf is a classic comfort food. To make things interesting, this recipe has a sweet and spicy glaze with brown sugar and spicy brown mustard. There's very little work involved, and essentially no clean-up, either!

Ingredients:

1 pound lean ground beef
⅔ cup bread crumbs
⅔ cup diced onion
6 sliced black olives
1 egg white
2 tbsp ketchup
2 fresh, chopped basil leaves
1 tsp minced garlic
½ tsp salt
Black pepper
¼ cup ketchup
1 tbsp brown sugar
1 tbsp spicy brown mustard

Directions:

1. Prepare a round, one-quart dish with a bit of olive oil.
2. Mix everything in the first ingredient list and form a loaf in the dish.
3. In a separate bowl, mix the brown sugar, ketchup, and spicy brown mustard together.
4. Brush on top of the meatloaf.
5. Cover the dish tightly with foil.
6. Pour one cup of water into the pressure cooker and lower in the trivet.
7. Place the meatloaf dish on top and close the Instant Pot lid.
8. Select MEAT/STEW, and then 45 minutes.
9. When the beep sounds, quick-release.
10. Carefully take out the hot dish.
11. Holding the meat in place, pour out any excess liquid.
12. Rest the meat before serving.

Nutritional Info (per serving): Calories - 261; Fat – 7.5; Fiber - 0; Carbs – 19.2; Protein - 25

Texas-Style Beef Chili

(Prep + Cook Time: 55 minutes | Servings: 4)

This chili is meaty. It's packed with ground beef, savory spices, and fresh vegetables, making it a very hearty dish.

Ingredients:

1 pound beef, grass-fed, organic
1 onion, large-sized, diced
1 green bell pepper, seeds removed and diced
1 tbsp fresh parsley, chopped
1 tbsp Worcestershire sauce
1 tsp garlic powder
1 tsp onion powder
1 tsp paprika
1 tsp sea salt
½ tsp ground black pepper
26 ounces tomatoes, finely chopped
4 carrots, large-sized, chopped into small pieces
4 tsp chili powder
Pinch cumin
For serving, optional:
Jalapenos, sliced
Onions, diced
Sour cream, dairy-free

Directions:

1. Press the SAUTE key. Add the ground beef into the instant pot and cook until browned.
2. Add the remaining Ingredients and mix well to combine. Lock the lid and close the steam valve.
3. Press CANCEL to stop the sauté function. Press MEAT/ STEW key.
4. When the timer beeps, let the pressure release naturally. Enjoy!

Nutritional Info (per serving): Calories - 308; Fat – 8.1; Fiber - 6; Carbs – 21.7; Protein – 37.8

Swedish Meatballs

(Prep + Cook Time: 20 minutes | Servings: 4)

Your family will surely love this simple and quick instant pot dish. The best part about this recipe, is you just dump all the ingredients in the pot. It's the meatball version of beef stroganoff.

Ingredients:

16 ounces egg noodles

1 ½ cups beef broth, low sodium

1 cup sour cream

1 cup milk

1 bag (24 Ounces) Johnsonville Home-style Meatballs, fully cooked or frozen

2 boxes (12 ounces) cream of mushroom soup (mix with 12 ounces water for both)

Directions:

1. Put the cream of mushroom soup, milk, beef broth, and water in the pot. Add the package of egg noodles.
2. In a single layer, layer the meatballs on top of the egg noodles. Cover and lock the lid.
3. Press the MANUAL key, set the pressure to HIGH, and set the timer for 12 minutes.
4. When there are only 2 minutes left of cooking time, turn the steam valve to VENTING. Unlock and carefully open the lid when all the steam is released.
5. Stir in 1 cup sour cream and mix thoroughly. Now you have dreamy, creamy, delicious Swedish meatballs.

Nutritional Info (per serving): Calories - 740; Fat – 45.4; Fiber – 3.4; Carbs – 52.1; Protein – 42.5

Pork and Lamb Recipes

Teriyaki Pork Tenderloin

(Prep + Cook Time: 30 minutes | Servings: 4)

This dish is kid-tested and approved. This will become your new favorite fast dinner. It only takes 30 minutes of actual cooking and the meat comes out juicy, tender, and super flavorful.

Ingredients:

2 pork tenderloins, cut into half

2 cups teriyaki sauce (if using a thick kind, thin it out some water so prevent it from burning on the bottom of the pot)

2 green onions, chopped

2 tbsp canola oil OR a similar oil

Generous amounts salt and pepper

Sesame seeds, toasted

Directions:

1. Press the SAUTE button of your Instant Pot and put the oil in the pot.
2. When the pot is hot, put about 1-2 tenderloins in the pot and lightly brown a few sides of the tenderloins.
3. When the meat is browned, lay the roast down and pour the sauce over the top of the tenderloins. Cover and lock the lid.
4. Press the MANUAL key, set the pressure to HIGH, and set the timer for 20 minutes.
5. When the Instant Pot timer beeps, release the pressure naturally for 10 minutes. Turn the steam valve to release remaining pressure.
6. Unlock and carefully open the lid. Slice the meat into pieces.
7. Serve with steamed broccoli and jasmine rice.
8. Garnish with chopped green onions and toasted sesame seeds.

Nutritional Info (per serving): Calories - 538; Fat – 20.2; Fiber – 0.7; Carbs – 45.9; Protein – 40.1

Pork Ribs BBQ

(Prep + Cook Time: 30 minutes | Servings: 4)

You can cook this delicious dish any night of the week. It's ready within minutes and not for hours.

Ingredients:

1 pork spare rib (about 6 pounds)

½ cup Knob Creek Bourbon (optional)

½ cup water

Barbecue sauce

Onion powder

Garlic powder Chipotle

Directions:

1. Set a steamer rack in the Instant Pot and pour in the water and bourbon.
2. Sprinkle the pork ribs with the onion powder, garlic, and chipotle.
3. Coil into a circle and vertically place on the steamer rack. Cover and lock the lid.
4. Press the MANUAL key, set the pressure to HIGH, and set the timer for 25 minutes.
5. When the Instant Pot timer beeps, release the pressure naturally for 15 minutes.
6. Turn the steam valve to release remaining pressure. Unlock and carefully open the lid.
7. Transfer the pork ribs on a baking sheet lined with foil and coat with barbecue sauce.
8. Broil for a couple minutes to caramelize the sauce. Cut the ribs in-between the bones. Serve with additional sauce.

Nutritional Info (per serving): Calories - 1968; Fat – 120.5; Fiber – 0; Carbs – 0; Protein – 180.2

Honey Pork Chops

(Prep + Cook Time: 25 minutes | Servings: 4)

This comforting Instant Pot pork chops recipe is savory and sweet. It's simple and needs only a couple of ingredients to make.

Ingredients:

2 pounds pork chops, boneless
2 tbsp Dijon mustard
¼ tsp cloves, ground
¼ tsp black pepper
¼ cups honey
½ tsp sea salt
½ tsp fresh ginger, peeled and minced
½ tsp cinnamon
½ tbsp maple syrup

Directions:

1. Sprinkle the pork chops with pepper and salt.
2. Put the seasoned pork in the pot.
3. Press the SAUTE key and brown both sides of the pork chops in the pot. In a bowl, combine the honey with the maple syrup, Dijon mustard, cloves, and cinnamon.
4. Pour the mix over the pork chops.
5. Press the CANCEL key to stop the sauté function. Cover and lock the lid. Press the MANUAL key, set the pressure to HIGH, and set the timer for 15 minutes.
6. When the Instant Pot timer beeps, release the pressure naturally or quickly. Unlock and carefully open the lid. Serve.

Nutritional Info (per serving): Calories - 804; Fat – 56.7; Fiber – 0.5; Carbs – 20.1; Protein – 51.4

Pork Chops With Mushroom Gravy

(Prep + Cook Time: 35 minutes | Servings: 4)

These pork chops are fork tender. The caramelized browned of pork chop bits from pan incorporates into the gravy, adding a delicious flavor into the dish. It's perfect over mashed potatoes.

Ingredients:
4 pork chops, bone-in thick
2 tbsp vegetable oil
1 can condensed cream of mushroom soup
1 ½ cups water
1 lemon
Pepper to taste

Directions:
1. Pat the pork chops dry and then liberally season with lemon pepper or your preferred seasoning.
2. Put the oil in the in the pot and press the SAUTE key.
3. When the oil starts to sizzle, brown both sides of the pork chops in the pot. When browned, transfer into a platter.
4. When all the pork chops are browned, pour the water in the pot to deglaze the pot.
5. Stir and scrape any browned bits off from the bottom of the pot.
6. Stir in the mushroom soup and then return the browned pork chops into the pot, along with any meat juices that accumulated on the platter.
7. Press the CANCEL key to stop the sauté function. Cover and lock the lid.
8. Press the MANUAL key, set the pressure to HIGH, and set the timer for 18 minutes.
9. When the Instant Pot timer beeps, release the pressure naturally for 10-15 minutes or until the valve drops.
10. Turn the steam valve to release remaining pressure. Unlock and carefully open the lid.
11. Transfer the pork chops into a large-sized serving bowl.
12. If needed, thicken the gravy in the pot with a slurry of flour and water.
13. Pour the thick gravy over the chops. Serve.

Nutritional Info (per serving): Calories - 381; Fat – 31.2; Fiber – 0; Carbs – 5.1; Protein – 19.2

Pork Fried Rice

(Prep + Cook Time: 40 minutes | Servings: 4)

Skip the takeout and make this classic yourself. It's a fast, tasty meal that's perfect for lunch leftovers the next day.

Ingredients:

3 cups + 2 tbsp water

2 cups white rice

8-ounces thin pork loin, cut into ½-inch slices

1 beaten egg

½ cup frozen peas

1 chopped onion

1 peeled and chopped carrot

3 tbsp olive oil

3 tbsp soy sauce

Salt + pepper

Directions:

1. Turn your Instant Pot to SAUTE.
2. Pour in 1 tablespoon of oil and cook the carrot and onion for 2 minutes.
3. Season the pork. Cook in the pot for 5 minutes.
4. Hit CANCEL and take out the onion, carrot, and pork.
5. Deglaze with the water. Add rice and a bit of salt. Lock the lid.
6. Hit RICE and cook for the default time.
7. When time is up, press CANCEL and wait 10 minutes.
8. Release any leftover steam.
9. Stir the rice, making a hollow in the middle so you can see the bottom of the pot.
10. Hit SAUTE and add 2 tablespoons of oil.
11. Add the egg in the hollow and whisk it around to scramble it while it cooks. When cooked, pour in peas, onion, carrot, and pork.
12. Stir until everything has warmed together.
13. Stir in soy sauce, press CANCEL, and serve.

Nutritional Info (per serving): Calories - 547; Fat – 2; Fiber – 3; Carbs – 81; Protein – 22

Pork Carnitas

(Prep + Cook Time: 60 minutes | Servings: 4)

This carnitas is very versatile. You can make a big batch and have a quick meal. You can serve this pork carnitas on top of a salad, quesadillas, burritos, or tacos.

Ingredients:

4 pounds pork roast
4 cloves garlic, minced
2 tsp salt
2 tbsp cumin
2 tbsp chili powder
1 tsp black pepper
1 tbsp oregano
1 tbsp ghee OR coconut oil
1 orange, cut in half
1 onion, chopped
1 jalapeno pepper, deseeded and diced
Small gluten-free OR corn tortillas

Directions:
1. Press the SAUTE key of the Instant Pot and wait until hot.
2. Combine the chili powder, cumin, oregano, pepper, and salt to make a rub.
3. Rub the pork the spice rub mix, coating all the surface of the meat and using all the seasoning.
4. Put the oil in the pot and add the pork. Sear each side of the pork for a couple of minutes until all the sides are beginning to get crispy.
5. Add the rest of the ingredients into the pot. Gently mix and spread out the ingredients with a spoon.
6. Squeeze the orange juice over the pork and add the orange back in in the pot to cook with the meat. Press the CANCEL key. Cover and lock the lid.

7. Press the MANUAL key, set the pressure to HIGH, and set the timer for 50 minutes.
8. When the Instant Pot timer beeps, release the pressure naturally for 10 minutes to let the meat absorb the flavor.
9. Turn the steam valve to release remaining pressure. Unlock and carefully open the lid.
10. Shred the pork carnitas and serve on quesadillas, tortillas, burritos, or top of a salad.
11. If serving on tortillas, top with avocado and sprinkle with cilantro and a dash of paprika.

Nutritional Info (per serving): Calories - 1033; Fat – 47.6; Fiber – 4.1; Carbs – 13.6; Protein – 131.4

Pork Cutlets With the Plum Sauce

(Prep + Cook Time: 40 minutes | Servings: 6)

You can substitute the fresh plums with the canned plums – the dish will save its incredible aroma and taste.

Ingredients:

12 oz ground pork
1/3 cup lemon juice
6 oz plums, pitted
1 tbsp sugar
1 tsp cilantro
½ tsp thyme
1 egg
1 tbsp cornstarch
1 tbsp ground ginger
1 tbsp olive oil
1 tbsp flour
1 tsp paprika

Directions:

1. Combine the ground pork with the cilantro, thyme, cornstarch, paprika, and egg.
2. Mix up the mixture carefully till you get homogenous mass.
3. Then make the medium cutlets from the ground meat mixture.
4. Pour the olive oil in the Instant Pot and add the pork cutlets. Cook the cutlets at the SAUTE mode for 10 minutes.
5. Stir the cutlets till all the sides are golden brown.
6. Meanwhile, put the plums in the blender and blend them until smooth. Then add sugar, ground ginger, flour, sugar, and lemon juice.
7. Blend the mixture for 1 minute more.
8. When the cutlets are cooked – pour the plum sauce in the Instant Pot.
9. Close the lid and cook the dish at the STEW mode for 10 minutes.
10. Then remove the pork cutlets from the Instant Pot, sprinkle them with the plum sauce.
11. Serve the dish hot!

Nutritional Info (per serving): Calories - 234; Fat – 9.7; Fiber – 1; Carbs – 14.5; Protein – 23

Cilantro Pork Tacos

(Prep + Cook Time: 45 minutes | Servings: 6)

These tacos should be served only hot. They are aromatic and very soft.

Ingredients:
1 tbsp cilantro
10 oz ground pork
1 tbsp tomato paste
1 red onion
1 tsp salt
1 tsp basil
1 tbsp butter
1 cup lettuce
7 oz corn tortilla
1 tsp paprika

Directions:
1. Combine the ground pork, salt, cilantro, paprika, and basil together in the mixing bowl.
2. Add butter and tomato paste. Stir the mixture well.
3. After this, place the ground pork mixture in the Instant Pot and close the lid.
4. Cook the dish at the MEAT mode for 27 minutes.
5. Meanwhile, chop the lettuce and peel the onion. Slice the onion.
6. When the meat is cooked – remove it from the Instant Pot and transfer in the corn tortillas.
7. Then add chopped lettuce and sliced onion. Wrap the tacos.
8. Serve the dish immediately.

Nutritional Info (per serving): Calories - 189; Fat – 6.5; Fiber – 3; Carbs – 17.5; Protein – 17

Pork Satay

(Prep + Cook Time: 35 minutes | Servings: 6)

The marinated meat pieces have a wonderful tender taste. You will enjoy and love the pork satay.

Ingredients:

12 oz pork loin

3 tbsp apple cider vinegar

1 tbsp olive oil

1 tbsp sesame oil

1 tsp turmeric

½ tsp cayenne pepper

1 tsp cilantro

1 tsp basil

1 tsp brown sugar

1 tsp soy sauce

11 tbsp fish sauce

Directions:
1. Chop the pork loin into the medium pieces.
2. Place the chopped pork lion in the mixing bowl. Sprinkle the meat with the apple cider vinegar, olive oil, sesame oil, turmeric, cayenne pepper, cilantro, basil, brown sugar, soy sauce, and fish sauce. Mix up the mixture.
3. Then screw the meat into the skewers.
4. Place the skewers in the Instant Pot.
5. Cook the pork satay for 25 minutes at the MEAT mode.
6. When the dish is cooked – remove the pork satay from the Instant Pot.
7. Chill the dish little.
8. Serve the pork satay immediately. Enjoy!

Nutritional Info (per serving): Calories - 214; Fat – 12; Fiber – 0; Carbs – 4.3; Protein – 21

Pulled pork

(Prep + Cook Time: 40 minutes | Servings: 8)

This pulled pork should be served with the toasted roll or French bread.

Ingredients:

2-pound pork shoulder
½ cup tomato paste
½ cup cream
¼ cup chicken stock
1 tbsp salt
1 tsp ground black pepper
1 tsp cayenne pepper
3 tbsp olive oil
1 tbsp lemon juice
1 tsp garlic powder
1 onion

Directions:

1. Peel the onion and transfer it to the blender.
2. Blend the onion till it is smooth. Pour the olive oil in the Instant Pot and add pork shoulder and roast the meat at the sauté mode for 10 minutes.
3. Then add tomato paste, cream, chicken stock, ground black pepper, cayenne pepper, lemon juice, and garlic powder.
4. Mix up the mixture and close the Instant Pot lid. Cook the dish at the pressure mode for 15 minutes.
5. When the time is over – remove the pork shoulder from the Instant Pot and shred it with the help of the folk.
6. After this, return the shredded pork back in the Instant Pot and mix up the mixture carefully.
7. Cook the dish at the manual mode for 2 minutes more.
8. Then transfer the cooked dish in the serving plate.
9. Serve the dish immediately.

Nutritional Info (per serving): Calories - 403; Fat – 28.5; Fiber – 1; Carbs – 6.3; Protein – 30

Ham and Peas (S&F)

(Prep + Cook Time: 50 minutes | Servings: 10)

This dish is a great recipe to make after New Year's Day. Each serving of this wonderful recipe is high in fiber, manganese, phosphorus, and thiamin, and very high in niacin and vitamin C.

Ingredients:

5 ounces ham, diced

1 pound dried peas, use black-eyed (rinse, but do not pre-soak)

6 ½ cups stock (vegetable, chicken, or ham)

6 ½ cups water mixed with

2 tbsp chicken bouillon

Directions:
1. Put all of the ingredients into the pot. Cover and lock the lid.
2. Press the MANUAL key, set the pressure to HIGH, and set the timer to 30 minutes.
3. When the Instant Pot timer beeps, press the CANCEL key and unplug the Instant Pot.
4. Let the pressure release naturally for 10-15 minutes or until the valve drops.
5. Unlock and carefully open the lid. Taste and season with salt and pepper as needed.

Note: The cooking time indicated for this dish cooked the peas well-done and soft, with a couple falling apart. If you want the peas to be more firm, then reduce the cooking time for a couple of minutes.

Nutritional Info (per serving): Calories - 85; Fat – 2.3; Fiber – 2.5; Carbs – 7.7; Protein – 8

Thyme Lamb (S&F)

(Prep + Cook Time: 55 minutes | Servings: 8)

The lamb that is cooked by this recipe needs only the fresh thyme – it will make the cooked dish aromatic.

Ingredients:
1 cup fresh thyme
1 tbsp olive oil
2-pound lamb
1 tsp oregano
1 tbsp ground black pepper
1 tsp paprika
¼ cup rice wine
1 tsp sugar
4 tbsp butter
¼ cup chicken stock
1 tbsp turmeric

Directions:
1. Chop the fresh thyme and combine it with the oregano, ground black pepper, paprika, rice wine, sugar, chicken stock, and turmeric.
2. Mix up the mixture.
3. Sprinkle the lamb with the spice mixture and stir it carefully.
4. After this, transfer the lamb mixture in the Instant Pot and add olive oil.
5. Close the Instant Pot lid and cook the dish at the MEAT mode for 45 minutes.
6. When the meat is cooked – remove it from the Instant Pot.
7. Chill the lamb little and slice it. Enjoy!

Nutritional Info (per serving): Calories - 384; Fat – 27.6; Fiber – 2; Carbs – 5.2; Protein – 29

Lamb Shanks

(Prep + Cook Time: 1 hour 10 minutes | Servings: 4)

This Instant Pot lamb shanks are infused with delicious flavors. The meat falls off the bone tender into a scrumptious tomato gravy.

Ingredients:

3 pounds lamb shanks
3 carrots, peeled and chopped
1 can (14 ounces) fire-roasted tomatoes
¼ tsp pepper
½ tsp salt
½ tsp crushed red pepper flakes
1 yellow onion, diced
1 tbsp tomato paste
1 tbsp coconut oil
1 tbsp balsamic vinegar
1 cup beef stock
3 stalks celery, diced
4 cloves garlic, minced Italian parsley, chopped, for garnish

Directions:

1. Sprinkle the lamb shanks with pepper and salt.
2. Press the SAUTE key of the Instant Pot and wait until hot.
3. Add the coconut oil and heat.
4. When the oil hot, cook the lamb shanks for about 8 to 10 or until all sides are browned. Transfer into a platter.
5. Add the garlic, onion, celery, and carrots in the pot.
6. Season with pepper and salt. Cook, frequently stirring, until the onion is translucent – be careful not to burn the garlic.
7. Add the fire-roasted tomatoes and the tomato paste. Stir to mix. Return the lamb shanks in the pot. Add the beef stock and balsamic vinegar.
8. Press the CANCEL key to stop the sauté function. Cover and lock the lid.

9. Press the MANUAL key, set the pressure to HIGH, and set the timer for 45 minutes.
10. When the Instant Pot timer beeps, release the pressure naturally for 10-15 minutes or until the valve drops.
11. Turn the steam valve to release remaining pressure. Unlock and carefully open the lid.
12. Transfer the lamb shanks in a serving plate. Ladle the sauce over the shanks.
13. Garnish with chopped fresh parsley.

Nutritional Info (per serving): Calories – 547; Fat – 28.8; Fiber – 3.4; Carbs – 13.3; Protein – 98.3

Lamb and Avocado Salad

(Prep + Cook Time: 45 minutes | Servings: 10)

The lamb and avocado salad is a nice solution for the nutritious lunch. You can substitute the lamb with any of your favorite meat.

Ingredients:

1 avocado, pitted
1 cucumber
8 oz lamb fillet
3 cups water
1 tsp salt
1 tsp chili pepper
3 tbsp olive oil
1 garlic clove
1 tsp basil
1 tbsp sesame oil
1 cup lettuce

Directions:

1. Place the lamb fillet in the Instant Pot and add water.
2. Sprinkle the mixture with the salt.
3. Peel the garlic clove and add it to the lamb mixture. Close the lid and cook the dish at the MEAT mode for 35 minutes.
4. Meanwhile, slice the cucumbers and chop the avocado. Combine the ingredients together in the mixing bowl.
5. Chop the lettuce roughly and add it to the mixing bowl.
6. After this, sprinkle the mixture with the chili pepper, olive oil, basil, and sesame oil.
7. When the meat is cooked – remove it from the Instant Pot and chill it well.
8. Chop the meat roughly and add it to the mixing bowl.
9. Mix up the salad carefully and transfer it to the serving bowl.
10. Serve the dish warm. Enjoy!

Nutritional Info (per serving): Calories - 203; Fat – 17.5; Fiber – 2; Carbs – 3.5; Protein – 9

Seafood Recipes

Quick Seafood Paella

(Prep + Cook Time: 55 minutes | Servings: 4)

Traditional cooking will multiple steps and hours to cook paella. With the Instant Pot, it's easy. Now you can make and enjoy paella anytime you want.

Ingredients:

For the fish stock:

6 cups water

4 white fish heads (I used cod)

2 carrots

1 celery

1 bay leaf

Bunch parsley with stems

For the paella:

1 ¾ cups seafood stock or vegetable stock

1 cup seafood mix (meaty white fish, squid, scallops)

2 cups mixed shellfish (clams, shrimp, and mussels)

2 cups rice, short-grain

1 green bell pepper, diced

1 red bell pepper, diced

1 yellow onion, medium-sized, diced

1/8 tsp ground turmeric

2 tsp sea salt

4 tbsp extra-virgin olive oil

Large pinch saffron threads

Directions:

1. Put all the fish stock ingredients in the Instant Pot.
2. Press MANUAL and set the timer for 5 minutes.
3. When the timer beeps, let the pressure release naturally. Transfer the fish stock in a heatproof container and set aside.

4. Wash and dry the inner pot. Return to the housing. Press the SAUTE key.
5. Add the olive oil and heat. When the oil is hot, add the onions and peppers, and sauté for about 4 minutes or until the onions are soft.
6. Stir in the rice, saffron, seafood, and sauté for 2 minutes.
7. Add h stock, salt, and turmeric, and stir to mix.
8. Arrange the shellfish on top – do not mix. Lock the lid and close the steam valve. Cook on HIGH pressure for 6 minutes.
9. When the timer is up, let the pressure release naturally for 15 minutes.
10. Open the steam valve to release any remaining pressure. Carefully open the lid.
11. Mix the paella, close the lid, and let stand for 1 minute. Serve!

Note: If you don't want to make your own fish stock, you can use vegetable stock instead. You can use avocado oil instead of olive oil to sauté the aromatic.

Nutritional Info (per serving): Calories – 665; Fat – 17.7; Fiber – 3.6; Carbs – 91.3; Protein – 33.3

Seafood Cranberries Plov

(Prep + Cook Time: 40 minutes | Servings: 4)

This delicious dish is fragrant and slightly sweet. It's a cranberry studded seafood dish with healthy carrots.

Ingredients:

1 package (16 ounces) frozen seafood blend, (I used Trader Joe's)
1 lemon, sliced
1 onion, large-sized, chopped
1 ½ cups basmati rice, organic
1 pepper, red or yellow, sliced
½ cup dried cranberries
2-3 tbsp butter
3 cups water
3-4 big shredded carrots
Salt and pepper, to taste

Directions:

1. Press the SAUTE key of the Instant Pot and wait until the word HOT appears on the display.
2. Put the butter in the pot. Add the onion, carrots, pepper, and cook stirring for about 5-7 minutes.
3. Stir in the rice, seafood blend, and cranberries.
4. Season generously and add 3 cups water.
5. Press RICE and lock the lid.
6. Just before servings, squeeze fresh squeezed lemon juice over the dish.

Nutritional Info (per serving): Calories – 430; Fat – 7.3; Fiber – 3.3; Carbs – 66.6; Protein – 21.4

Shrimp Creole

(Prep + Cook Time: 20 minutes | Servings: 4)

This dish is easy to make, but it's flavorful. It's a healthy, light dish when you are on a diet. Serve over hot cooked rice.

Ingredients:

1 can (28 ounces) crushed tomatoes
1 pound jumbo shrimp, frozen, peeled and deveined
1 onion, medium-sized, chopped
1 tsp thyme
¼ tsp cayenne pepper, or to taste
2 cloves garlic, minced
2 stalks celery, diced
1 bay leaf
1 bell pepper, diced
1 tbsp tomato paste
1 tsp salt
½ tsp pepper
2 tsp olive oil

Directions:

1. Press the SAUTE key of the Instant Pot. Add the oil and heat.
2. When the oil is hot, add the vegetables and sauté for 3 minutes or until the veggies starts to soften.
3. Add the tomato paste. Stir and cook for 1 minute.
4. Add the crushed tomatoes, shrimp, seasoning, and stir to combine.
5. Press MANUAL, set the pressure to HIGH, and set the timer to 1 minute.
6. When the timer beeps, quick release the pressure.
7. Carefully open the lid. If the shrimp is not fully cooked, press the SAUTE key and cook the shrimp for 1 minute, constantly stirring.
8. Serve over rice.

Nutritional Info (per serving): Calories – 264; Fat – 4.5; Fiber – 7.9; Carbs – 24.4; Protein – 31.6

Grispy Skin Salmon Fillet

(Prep + Cook Time: 20 minutes | Servings: 2)

This weeknight-friendly dish takes 15 minutes to cook. It's easy, healthy, but flavorful.

Ingredients:

2 salmon fillets, frozen (1-inch thickness)
1 cup tap water, running cold
2 tbsp olive oil
Salt and pepper, to taste

Directions:

1. Pour 1 cup water in the Instant Pot.
2. Set the steamer rack and put the salmon fillets in the rack. Lock the lid and close the steamer valve.
3. Press MANUAL, set the pressure on LOW, and set the timer for 1 minute.
4. When the timer beeps, turn off the pot and quick release the pressure.
5. Carefully open the lid. Remove the salmon fillets and pat them dry using paper towels.
6. Over medium-high heat, preheat a skillet.
7. Grease the salmon fillet skins with 1 tablespoon olive oil and generously season with black pepper and salt.
8. When the skillet is very hot, with the skin side down, put the salmon fillet in the skillet.
9. Cook for 1-2 minutes until the skins are crispy.
10. Transfer the salmon fillets into serving plates and serve with your favorite side dishes.
11. This dish is great with rice and salad.

Note: You can use a nonstick skillet to make sure the skin does not stick to the skillet. If you do not like the skin on your salmon, you can remove it after pressure cooking. Increase the cooking time to 2 minutes.

Nutritional Info (per serving): Calories – 356; Fat – 25; Fiber – 0; Carbs – 0

Dijon Salmon (S&F)

(Prep + Cook Time: 10 minutes | Servings: 2)

This is the simplest fish dish that you can cook in your Instant Pot. Plus, it takes only 2 ingredients to make.

Ingredients:

2 pieces firm fish fillets or steaks, such as salmon, scrod, cod, or halibut

1 cup water

1 tsp

Dijon mustard per fish fillet

Steamer basket or trivet

Directions:

1. On the fleshy portion of the fish fillets, spread 1 teaspoon of Dijon mustard over.
2. Pour 1 cup of water into the Instant Pot.
3. Set the steamer basket or trivet in the pot.
4. With the skin side faced down, put the fish fillets in the steamer basket/ trivet. Cover and lock the lid.
5. Press MANUAL and set the timer according to the thickest fish fillet.
6. When the timer beeps, turn the steam valve to quick release the pressure. Serve.

Nutritional Info (per serving): Calories – 191; Fat – 1,7; Fiber – 0; Carbs – 0.1; Protein – 41.2

Tuna and Pasta Casserole

(Prep + Cook Time: 10 minutes | Servings: 2)

This tuna casserole in the Instant Pot is very easy and quick to make. All you have to do is to put everything in the pot and cook - dinner in less than half an hour!

Ingredients:

1 can cream of mushroom soup
1 cup cheddar cheese, shredded
1 cups frozen peas
2 cans tuna
2 ½ cups macaroni pasta
½ tsp salt
½ tsp pepper
3 cups water

Directions:

1. Mix the soup with the water in the Instant Pot. Except for the cheese, add the rest of the ingredients.
2. Stir to combine. Lock the lid and turn the steam valve to SEALING. Press MANUAL, set the pressure to HIGH, and set the timer for 4 minutes.
3. When the timer beeps, turn the steam valve to VENTING to quickly release the pressure. Unlock and open the lid.
4. Sprinkle the cheese on top. Close the lid and let sit for 5 minutes or until the cheese is melted and the sauce is thick.

Nutritional Info (per serving): Calories – 877; Fat – 30.7; Fiber – 7.9; Carbs – 96; Protein – 51.9

Fish in Orange Ginger Sauce

(Prep + Cook Time: 20 minutes | Servings: 4)

This dish combined the subtle flavor of fish and the rich flavors of the ginger and orange to make a very delectable meal. In less than 20 minutes, you have a delicious and healthy meal.

Ingredients:

4 pieces white fish fillets

3-4 spring onions

1 piece (thumb-sized) ginger, chopped

1 orange, zested and then juiced

1 cup white wine or fish stock

Olive oil

Salt and pepper

Directions:

1. Using a paper towel, pat the fish fillets dry. Rub the fillets with the olive oil and then season them lightly.
2. Add the white wine/ fish stock, orange zest, orange juice, ginger, and spring onion into the Instant Pot.
3. Set a steamer basket in the pot and then put the fish in the steamer basket. Close and lock the lid.
4. Press MANUAL and set the timer to 7 minutes.
5. Serve on top of an undressed garden salad.
6. The sauce will serve as the dressing.

Nutritional Info (per serving): Calories – 268; Fat – 1.7; Fiber – 1.6; Carbs – 8.8; Protein – 41.9

Wild Alaskan Cod In The Pot

(Prep + Cook Time: 15 minutes | Servings: 2)

This dish is simple, but it makes a great dinner. Especially if you pair it with steamed carrots and pretzel rolls.

Ingredients:

1 large filet wild Alaskan cod (the big fillets can feed easily 2-3 people)
1 cup cherry tomatoes
Salt and pepper, to taste
Your choice of seasoning
2 tbsp butter
Olive oil

Directions:

1. Choose an ovenproof dish that will fit your Instant Pot.
2. Put the tomatoes in the dish.
3. Cut the large fish fillet into 2-3 serving pieces. Lay them on top of the tomatoes.
4. Season the fish with salt, pepper, and your choice of seasoning.
5. Top each fillet with 1 tablespoon butter and drizzle with a bit of olive oil Put 1 cup water in the Instant Pot and set a trivet.
6. Place the dish on the trivet. Lock the lid and close the steam valve.
7. Press MANUAL and set the timer for 5 minutes if using thawed fish or for 9 minutes if using frozen fish.
8. When the timer beeps, let the pressure release naturally. Enjoy!

Nutritional Info (per serving): Calories – 832; Fat – 17.5; Fiber – 1.1; Carbs – 3.5; Protein – 156.2

Cod Chowder

(Prep + Cook Time: 40 minutes | Servings: 6)

The best part about this dish is that you can cook the fish and make the fish chowder in the same Instant Pot. You can use any soft white fish your desire or omit the mushrooms, if you don't have any on hand.

Ingredients:

2 pounds cod
4 cups potatoes, peeled and diced
4 cups chicken broth
2 tbsp butter
½ mushrooms, sliced
½ cup flour
1 tsp old bay seasoning (or more)
1 cup onion, chopped
1 cup half-and-half OR heavy cream OR 1 can evaporated milk
1 cup clam juice
4-6 bacon slices, optional
Salt and pepper, to taste

Directions:

1. Pour 1 cup water into the Instant Pot and set a trivet. Put the cod on the trivet. Close and lock the lid.
2. Press MANUAL, set the pressure to HIGH, and set the timer for 9 minutes.
3. Transfer the cod onto a large-sized plate. With a fork or a knife, cut the fish into large chunks. Set aside.
4. Remove the trivet and pour the liquid out from the inner pot. Return the inner pot into the housing.
5. Press the SAUTE key. Add the butter, onion, and mushrooms; sauté for 2 minutes or until soft.
6. Add the chicken broth and the potatoes.
7. Press the CANCEL key to stop the sauté function. Close and lock the lid.

8. Press the MANUAL key, set the pressure to HIGH, and set the timer for 8 minutes.
9. When the timer beeps, turn the steam valve to quick release the pressure.
10. Stir in the seasoning, pepper, salt, and fish. In a bowl, mix the clam juice with the flour until well blended.
11. Pour the mix into the pot. Turn off the Instant Pot.
12. Add the half-and-half and stir well until blended. Serve with fresh baked buttered rolls.

Notes: If you are using bacon, cook the bacon until crisp and then transfer into a paper towel lined plate. Add the onions and the mushrooms, cooking them in the bacon fat before adding the broth and potatoes.

Nutritional Info (per serving): Calories – 474; Fat – 16.3; Fiber – 3.3; Carbs – 32.4; Protein – 46.9

Tilapia bites

(Prep + Cook Time: 20 minutes | Servings: 8)

You can your favorite aromatic herbs in the batter to make the dish smell gorgeous.

Ingredients:

3 eggs
½ cup half and half
1 tsp salt
1-pound tilapia fillets
1 tsp red pepper
1 tbsp lemon juice
3 tbsp olive oil
1 tsp coriander
1 tsp cinnamon
½ lemon

Directions:
1. Beat the eggs in the bowl and whisk them with the help of the hand whisker.
2. After this, add salt, red pepper, and half and half in the whisked eggs mixture. Stir it.
3. Grate the lemon and squeeze the juice from it.
4. Chop the tilapia fillets into the big cubes.
5. Sprinkle the fish with the coriander and cinnamon. Stir the mixture. Spray the Instant Pot with the olive oil inside.
6. Dip the tilapia cubes in the egg mixture. Then transfer the fish in the Instant Pot.
7. SAUTE the fish for 4 minutes on the each side or till you get golden brown color.
8. Then transfer the cooked tilapia bites in the paper towel and chill the dish.
9. Serve the dish!

Nutritional Info (per serving): Calories – 158; Fat – 9.9; Fiber – 0; Carbs – 2.31; Protein – 15

Spicy Lemony Salmon

(Prep + Cook Time: 10 minutes | Servings: 4)

This dish is ready with little time and little effort. The salmon comes out deliciously moist, flaky, and just a bit spicy.

Ingredients:

3-4 pieces (1-inch thick) salmon fillets, wild sockeye

1-2 tbsp assorted chili pepper (I used Nanami Togarashi)

1 lemon, sliced

1 lemon, juiced

1 cup water

Salt and pepper, to taste

Directions:

1. Season the salmon fillets with the lemon juice, salt, pepper, and Nanami Togarashi.
2. Pour 1 cup water in the instant pot and set the steam rack in the pot.
3. Place the salmon fillets on the rack, arranging them in a single layer, if possible, without overlapping.
4. Pour any leftover lemon juice and seasoning over the fillets. Lock the lid and close the steam valve.
5. Press MANUAL and set the timer for 5 minutes. Reduce the time by 1 minute for every 1/4-inch thinner fillets and 1 minute more for every 1/4-inch thicker fillet.
6. When the timer beeps, release the pressure quickly. Carefully open the lid and transfer the fillets into a serving plate. Enjoy!

Notes: You can find Nanami Togarashi in the Asian section of the grocery store. If you want a spicier dish, sprinkle a bit of red pepper flakes over the fillets before cooking.

Nutritional Info (per serving): Calories – 182; Fat – 8.1; Fiber – 1; Carbs – 3.1; Protein – 25.6

Soup Recipes

In the Instant Pot, you will cook incredibly tasty, thick and fragrant soups. The recipes below will help you master the art of making soups to any taste easily and quickly.

Simple Chicken Soup

(Prep + Cook Time: 50 minutes | Servings: 4)

With just six ingredients, you can make a simple and delicious chicken soup that's perfect for when you're feeling under the weather. No need to buy the canned stuff anymore!

Ingredients:

16-ounces water

16-ounces chicken stock

2 frozen, boneless chicken breasts

4 medium-sized potatoes

Three peeled carrots

½ big diced onion

Salt and pepper

Directions:

1. Put everything into the pressure cooker, including salt and pepper.
2. Turn on your Instant Pot by selecting MANUAL, and then 35 minutes on HIGH pressure.
3. When time is up, turn off the cooker and wait 15 minutes for the pressure to come down by itself.
4. Carefully open the cooker, stir, and serve!

Nutritional Info (per serving): Calories – 72; Fiber – 0; Carbs – 7; Protein – 5

Chicken Tortilla Soup

(Prep + Cook Time: 30 minutes | Servings: 4)

Sometimes the classic chicken noodle soup needs a bit of a kick. This zesty chicken tortilla soup is the answer. It's super easy with the Instant Pot's "Soup" setting and full of great ingredients like tomato, beans, corn, and of course, tortillas.

Ingredients:
2, 6-inch corn tortillas cut into 1-inch squares
3-4 cups chicken broth
3 chicken breasts
1 big, chopped tomato
1 chopped onion
2 minced garlic cloves
15 ounces of black beans
1 cup frozen corn
2 tbsp chopped cilantro
1 bay leaf
1 tbsp olive oil
2 tsp chili powder
1 tsp ground cumin
¼ tsp ground cayenne pepper

Directions:
1. Turn on the Instant Pot to SAUTE.
2. Pour in the olive oil and cook the onion while stirring until soft.
3. Add the cilantro, garlic, and tortillas.
4. Stir and wait 1 minute.
5. Add the black beans, corn, tomato, 3 cups of broth, chicken, and spices.
6. Turn off the SAUTE function and close the lid.
7. Switch over to SOUP mode and adjust the time to just 4 minutes.
8. When time is up, quick-release the pressure.
9. Carefully take out the chicken and shred before returning back to the pot. Stir everything well.
10. Serve with cilantro, cheese, lime juice, and any other toppings you enjoy.

Nutritional Info (per serving): Calories – 200; Fat – 7; Fiber – 9; Carbs – 24; Protein – 7

Bean Soup

(Prep + Cook Time: 65 minutes | Servings: 6)

The cannellini beans make the soup aromatic and with the gorgeous taste! You will love this dish from the first sip!

Ingredients:

1 cup cannellini beans

7 cups water

1 cup dill

4 tbsp salsa

1 jalapeno pepper

1/3 cup cream

2 tsp salt

1 tsp white pepper

1 white onions

1 sweet red pepper

1-pound chicken fillet

1 tsp soy sauce

Directions:

1. Place the cannellini beans in the Instant Pot.
2. Chop the chicken fillet and add it in the Instant Pot too.
3. Add water and cook the beans at the PRESSURE mode for 35 minutes.
4. Meanwhile, chop the dill and jalapeno peppers. Slice the onions and chop the sweet red peppers.
5. Add the vegetables to bean mixture and close the lid. Set the Instant Pot mode SOUP and cook the dish for 15 minutes more.
6. Then sprinkle the soup with the cream, salsa, white pepper, and soy sauce. Stir the soup carefully and cook it for 5 minutes more.
7. Remove the soup from the Instant Pot and let it chill little.
8. Ladle the soup into the serving bowls. Enjoy!

Nutritional Info (per serving): Calories – 188; Fat – 10.3; Fiber – 2; Carbs – 17.3; Protein – 7

Spiced-Carrot Chilled Soup (VEG)

(Prep + Cook Time: 1 hour 40 minutes | Servings: 4)

Cold soups aren't super common anymore, but they're a great option for really hot days when you want something really refreshing that isn't a drink or dessert.

Ingredients:

2 pounds trimmed, peeled, and chopped carrots

3 tbsp olive oil

Salt to taste

Dukkah to taste

Water as needed

Directions:

1. Put carrots in your Instant Pot with ½ cup of water.
2. Seal the lid. Press MANUAL and adjust time to 30 minutes.
3. When time is up, press CANCEL and quick-release the pressure.
4. Remove carrots and blend with olive oil until smooth.
5. Pour soup through a sieve to get a really smooth texture.
6. Add water if necessary to get the right consistency.
7. Add salt to taste before storing in the fridge until chill.
8. Before serving, whisk and sprinkle on dukkah.

Note: Dukkah is a spice blend made from sesame seeds, cumin, salt, pepper, coriander, and hazelnuts. You can find it online, or at Trader Joe's and Whole Foods.

Nutritional Info (per serving): Calories – 159; Fat – 12; Fiber – 4; Carbs – 15; Protein – 2

Cheddar Broccoli and Potato Soup

(Prep + Cook Time: 25 minutes | Servings: 4)

This classic soup takes less than 30 minutes to make from start to finish.

Ingredients:

1 broccoli head, medium-sized, broken into large florets
1 cup cheddar cheese, shredded
1 cup half and half
2 cloves garlic, crushed
2 pounds Yukon Gold Potatoes, peeled and then cut into small chunks
2 tbsp butter
4 cups vegetable broth
Chives or green onion, chopped, for garnish
Salt and pepper, to taste

Directions:

1. Press the SAUTE key. When the pot is hot, add the butter and the garlic, and sauté for 1 minute or until the garlic starts to brown.
2. Add the potatoes, broccoli, broth, and season with a bit of salt and pepper. Lock the lid and close the steam valve. Cook for 5 minutes on HIGH.
3. When the timer beeps, press CANCEL and let the pressure release naturally for 10 minutes. Open the steam valve to release remaining pressure.
4. Add the half-and-half and ½ cup cheddar cheese. Using an immersion blender, blend until smooth.
5. Alternatively, you can blend in batches in a large-sized blender. If you want a thinner soup, just add more broth.
6. Season with salt and pepper to taste.
7. Serve hot with remaining cheddar.

Nutritional Info (per serving): Calories – 522; Fat – 35.7; Fiber – 2.7; Carbs – 23.8; Protein – 27.7

Split Pea Soup (VEG, S&F)

(Prep + Cook Time: 55 minutes | Servings: 6)

This soup mimics the smoky flavor of ham without any ham in it. However, if you want meat in your dish, you can add some cubed ham or ham hock in the pot.

Ingredients:

1 bay leaf
1 pound split peas
1 yellow onion, diced
½ tbsp smoked paprika
¼ tsp thyme
2 cloves garlic, minced
2 tbsp coconut oil (butter or your choice of oil)
3 carrots, sliced
3 stalks celery, sliced
6 cups vegetable broth
Fresh ground pepper

Directions:

1. Put the onion, celery, carrots, and garlic in the pot. Add the rest of the ingredients.
2. Lock the lid and close the steam valve. Press MANUAL and set the timer to 15 minutes.
3. When the timer beeps, let the pressure release naturally. Open the steam valve to release any remaining pressure in the pot and carefully open the lid.
4. Stir the soup, taste, and adjust seasoning as needed.
5. Serve hot with crusty bread.

Nutritional Info (per serving): Calories – 360; Fat – 6.9; Fiber – 20.9; Carbs – 52.3; Protein – 24.1

Sweet Potato Soup (VEG)

(Prep + Cook Time: 35 minutes | Servings: 4)

When you are tired after a day's work, here is a simple yet delicious soup to warm your tired bones. Each serving is low in cholesterol, high in fiber, iron, manganese, niacin, and potassium, and very high in vitamins A, B6, and C.

Ingredients:

6 carrots, peeled and diced

3-4 large red sweet potatoes, peeled and diced

1 whole onion, chopped

3-4 cloves garlic, chopped

2 tbsp butter

½ tsp thyme

½ tsp ground sage

1 quart vegetarian broth

Salt and pepper to taste

Directions:

1. Set the Instant Pot to SAUTE. Put the butter in and then add the garlic, onion, and carrots. Sauté until the onions are translucent.
2. Add the sweet potatoes, broth, and seasonings.
3. Press CANCEL. Close and lock the lid. Press MANUAL. Set the pressure to HIGH and set the timer for 20 minutes.
4. When the timer beeps, quick release the pressure. Carefully open the lid and stir the soup to blend.
5. With an immersion blender, blend until soft and serve.

Nutritional Info (per serving): Calories – 230; Fat – 7.4; Fiber – 6.2; Carbs – 33.5; Protein – 8.1

Quinoa Soup (VEG, S&F)

(Prep + Cook Time: 40 minutes | Servings: 6)

This is the easiest soup you'll ever make. You literally just throw everything in the Instant Pot and step back. The quinoa adds a different flavor and consistency than the usual noodles

Ingredients:

3 cups boiling water

2 bags of frozen mixed veggies (12 oz)

1 15 oz can of white beans

1 15 oz can of fire-roasted diced tomatoes

1 15 oz can of pinto beans

¼ cup rinsed quinoa

1 tbsp dried basil

1 tbsp minced garlic

1 tbsp hot sauce

½ tbsp dried oregano

Dash of salt

Dash of black pepper

Directions:

1. Put everything in the Instant Pot and stir. Close and seal the lid.
2. Select MANUAL and set time to 2 minutes on HIGH pressure.
3. When time is up, press CANCEL and quick-release the pressure.
4. When all the pressure is gone, open the cooker and season to taste. Serve.

Note: The reason the time range is so wide is because it can take between 15-20 minutes for the Instant Pot to reach pressure if you're using frozen veggies. Using boiling water helps with that, and if you use fresh veggies, it takes very little time to get to pressure)

Nutritional Info (per serving): Calories – 201; Fat – 1.1; Fiber – 11; Carbs – 37; Protein – 11

Turkish Soup

(Prep + Cook Time: 15 minutes | Servings: 2)

This simple soup has just the right amount of spices without being overwhelming for those with most delicate palates. It's thick and rich, but not too hearty. It would be a great option for lunch.

Ingredients:

1 cup red lentils
1 chopped carrot
1 chopped potato
1 chopped onion
½ cup celery
3 minced garlic cloves
½ tbsp rice
3 tsp olive oil
½ tsp paprika
½ tsp coriander
Salt to taste

Directions:

1. Turn your Instant Pot to SAUTE and add oil.
2. While that heats up, prep your veggies.
3. When oil is hot, cook the garlic for a few minutes until fragrant. Rinse off the rice and lentils, and put them in the Instant Pot.
4. Add 2 ½ cups of water, paprika, salt, and veggies. Close and seal the lid.
5. Select MANUAL and cook on HIGH pressure for 10 minutes.
6. When time is up, press CANCEL and quick-release.
7. Let the mixture cool for a little while before pureeing in a blender. Serve.

Nutritional Info (per serving): Calories – 531; Fat – 9; Fiber – 10; Carbs – 73; Protein – 29

Vegetable Recipes

Breakfast Potato Hash (VEG)

(Prep + Cook Time: 20 minutes | Servings: 6)

This hash combines the goodness of potatoes and the intensely sweet flavor of sweet potatoes into a savory, satisfying breakfast or brunch.

Ingredients:

1 large sweet potato, diced larger than the potatoes since they cook faster (about 1 cup)

1 large potato, diced to about ½-inch cubes (about 1 cup)

1 cup bell pepper, chopped (about 2 peppers)

1 clove garlic, minced

1 tbsp olive oil

1 tsp cumin

1 tsp paprika

½ tsp black pepper

½ tsp kosher salt

½ cup water Pinch cayenne

Directions:

1. Toss the veggies with the oil and the spices.
2. Add the mix into the Instant Pot and then add the 1/2 cup water in the pot.
3. Set the pressure to HIGH and the timer to 0 minutes.
4. When the timer beeps, turn the valve to release pressure naturally.
5. Open the pot and press the SAUTÉ button. Sauté for about 5 to 6 minutes or until the potato cubes begin to brown.
6. Serve.

Nutritional Info (per serving): Calories – 393; Fat – 7.9; Fiber – 8.7; Carbs – 55.6; Protein – 6.5

Baked Potatoes (VEG, S&F)

(Prep + Cook Time: 15 minutes | Servings: 8)

Are you tired of waiting for your baked potatoes to cook? Cook them in an Instant Pot and they will come out perfectly baked every time!

Ingredients:

5 pounds potatoes, peeled, if desired, chopped into roughly the same size

1 cup water, for the pot

Directions:

1. Pour the water into the Instant Pot container and then insert a steam rack.
2. Put the potatoes in the rack.
3. Close and lock the lid and make sure that the steam release valve is sealed. Press MANUAL and set the timer to 10 minutes.
4. When the timer beeps at the end of the cooking cycle, let the pressure release naturally for about 20 minutes.
5. Open the steam release valve to release any pressure remaining in the pot.
6. Serve and enjoy.

Nutritional Info (per serving): Calories – 156; Fat – 0.2; Fiber – 5.4; Carbs – 35.6; Protein – 3.8

Sweet Potatoes (VEG, S&F)

(Prep + Cook Time: 25 minutes | Servings: 6)

These veggies are very nutritious and versatile. They are creamy, tender, and make an excellent substitute for potatoes.

Ingredients:

6 sweet potatoes, medium-sized (about 150 grams each)

2 cups water, for the pot

Directions:

1. Wash the sweet potatoes clean and prick.
2. Pour 2 cups of water into the Instant Pot and put the steamer rack.
3. Layer the sweet potatoes on the rack.
4. Close and lock the lid. Press the MANUAL, set the pressure to HIGH, and the timer to 10 minutes.
5. When the timer beeps, turn the valve for quick pressure release.
6. Let the sweet potatoes cool and serve or store in an airtight container for up to 5 days.

Notes: If you are using large-sized sweet potatoes, set the timer to 12-15 minutes.

Nutritional Info (per serving): Calories – 177; Fat – 0.3; Fiber – 6.2; Carbs – 41.8; Protein – 2.3

Garlicky Mashed Potatoes

(Prep + Cook Time: 20 minutes | Servings: 4)

This ultra-creamy and super healthy Instant Pot mashed potatoes is absolutely scrumptious. Each serving has no cholesterol, high in manganese, potassium, and vitamin B6, and very high in vitamin C.

Ingredients:

4 medium russet, yellow finn or yukon gold potatoes

¼ cup parsley, chopped

½ cup milk, non-dairy

1 cup vegetable broth

6 cloves garlic, peeled and cut in half Salt

Directions:

1. Cut each potato into 8-12 chunks. Put into the Instant Pot.
2. Add the broth and the garlic.
3. Close and lock the lid. Press manual and set the timer to 4 minutes.
4. When the timer beeps, turn the valve to VENTING to quick release the pressure.
5. With a hand blender or a masher, mash the potatoes.
6. Depending on the consistency you want, add all the soymilk or just the amount you need.
7. Add salt taste and then add the parsley, stir to combine. If desired, add pepper.
8. Serve hot.

Nutritional Info (per serving): Calories – 234; Fat – 7.8; Fiber – 6; Carbs – 37.1; Protein – 5.9

Coconut Butter Garlic New Potatoes (VEG)

(Prep + Cook Time: 10 minutes | Servings: 2)

This classic dish is packed with delicious flavors of fresh herbs, garlic, and potatoes. This recipe is very simple and easy to make – just put all the ingredients in the pot and cook.

Ingredients:

1.1 lb potatoes

3 tbsp coconut butter

Handful fresh herbs

Salt and pepper

2/3 cup water

Directions:

1. Pour the water in the Instant Pot and set a steamer dish in the pot. Put the new potatoes in the steamer dish.
2. Add the fresh herbs, garlic, coconut butter, and a generous sprinkle of pepper and salt. Cover and lock the lid.
3. Press the MANUAL key, set the pressure to HIGH, and set the timer for 4 minutes. When the Instant Pot timer beeps, keep warm for 5 minutes.
4. Quick release the pressure.
5. When the potatoes are cool enough, transfer into a serving bowl and discard the excess coconut butter mixture.
6. Serve with additional fresh herbs, such as rosemary, parsley, chives, or whatever you have on hand.

Nutritional Info (per serving): Calories –279 ; Fat – 21; Fiber – 9.4; Carbs – 44.4; Protein – 5.4

Steamed Broccoli (VEG)

(Prep + Cook Time: 10 minutes | Servings: 2)

Broccoli is a powerhouse of nutrients. To mention a few, each serving of this dish is high in calcium, iron, magnesium, pantothenic acid, phosphorus, riboflavin, selenium, and thiamin, and very high in fiber, manganese, potassium, and vitamins A, B6, and C.

Ingredients:

2-3 cups broccoli florets

¼ cup water

A bowl with ice and cold water

Directions:

1. Pour the water into the Instant Pot container.
2. Put the steamer insert in the pot. Place the broccoli in the steamer.
3. Press MANUAL, set the pressure to HIGH, and the timer to 0 minutes.
4. Carefully watch the pot. Ready the bowl with iced water.
5. One the timer beeps after the end of the cooking cycle, immediately open the valve to quick pressure release.
6. Remove the steamer insert and then put the broccoli in the ice bath to stop cooking and helps keep the broccoli's bright green color.

Nutritional Info (per serving): Calories – 31; Fat – 0.3; Fiber – 2.4; Carbs – 6; Protein – 2.5

Pumpkin Puree (VEG)

(Prep + Cook Time: 30 minutes | Servings: 6)

Cooking it in an Instant Pot greatly reduces the time to 15 minutes. Of course, you can cook more in the oven, but when in a hurry, Instant Pot is the best way.

Ingredients:

2 pounds small-sized sugar pumpkin or pie pumpkin, halved and seeds scooped out

½ cup water

Directions:

1. Pour the water into the Instant Pot and set the steamer rack.
2. Put the pumpkin halves on the rack. Set the pressure to HIGH and the timer to 13 or 15 minutes.
3. When the timer beeps, turn the valve to quick release the pressure. Let the pumpkin cool.
4. When cool enough to handle scoop out the flesh into a bowl.
5. Puree using an immersion blender or puree in a blender.

Note: You can stir pumpkin into your oatmeal, use it to make a dessert, stir some with an applesauce for instant pumpkin applesauce, mix with softened butter with some sugar and spices like cinnamon, nutmeg, or cloves to make a compound butter for biscuits, blend it to make a creamy soup, and much more.

Nutritional Info (per serving): Calories – 51; Fat – 0.4; Fiber – 4.4; Carbs – 12.2; Protein – 1.7

Zucchini and Mushrooms (VEG)

(Prep + Cook Time: 20 minutes | Servings: 6)

This fast and easy dish has no cholesterol, low in saturated fat, high in iron, manganese, niacin, pantothenic acid, phosphorus, and potassium, and very high in fiber, riboflavin, and vitamins.

Ingredients:

8-12 oz mushrooms, sliced or separated depending on type of mushroom
4 medium zucchini, cut into ½-inch slices (about 8 cups)
1 can (15 ounce) crushed or diced tomatoes with juice
1 large sprig fresh basil, sliced
1 tbsp extra-virgin olive oil
½ tsp black pepper, or to taste
½ tsp salt, or to taste
2 cloves garlic, minced
1 ½ cup onions, diced

Directions:

1. Press the SAUTE button of the Instant Pot. Add the olive oil and heat.
2. Add the garlic, onions, and mushrooms; cook, frequently stirring, until the onions are soft and the mushrooms lose their moisture.
3. Add the basil and sprinkle with the salt and pepper. Sauté for 5 minutes until the mushrooms are soft.
4. Add the zucchini, stir. Add the tomatoes with the juices over the zucchini; do not stir.
5. Close and lock the lid. Press the MANUAL button. Set the pressure to LOW and the timer to 1 minute.
6. When the timer beeps, turn the steam valve to quick release the pressure. Carefully remove the cover.
7. If the zucchini are still a little undercooked, just cover the pot and let rest for 1 minutes to allow the zucchinis to soften.
8. Serve over pasta, rice, baked potatoes, or polenta. If desired, you can stir a can of white beans.

Nutritional Info (per serving): Calories – 96; Fat – 2.8; Fiber – 5; Carbs – 15.2; Protein – 5.6

Ricotta-Stuffed Zucchini

(Prep + Cook Time: 10 minutes | Servings: 6)

Creamy ricotta makes a delicious filling for fresh summer zucchini. You mix the ricotta with breadcrumbs, nutmeg, thyme, and an egg yolk, and then stuff small logs of zucchini. The stuffed veggies cook for just 5 minutes in a bath of crushed tomatoes, oil, and onion, and you have the perfect appetizer ready to go.

Ingredients:

3 big zucchinis
1 ¾ cups crushed tomatoes
1 cup ricotta
1 yellow onion
½ cup breadcrumbs
2 tbsp olive oil
1 tbsp minced fresh oregano
1 large egg yolk
2 tsp minced garlic
2 tsp fresh thyme
¼ tsp grated nutmeg
Salt + pepper

Directions:

1. Mix breadcrumbs, ricotta, egg yolk, nutmeg, and thyme in a bowl.
2. Prepare the zucchini by cutting them into 2-inch long pieces. With a melon baller, hollow out the middles with about ¼-inch flesh on the sides and ½-inch on the bottom, so they don't fall apart.
3. Stuff 2 tablespoons of the ricotta mixture into the hollows.
4. Turn your Instant Pot to SAUTE, and cook onion until soft.
5. Add garlic and cook another 30 seconds.
6. Add oregano, tomatoes, salt, and pepper.
7. Put the zucchinis in the cooker, stuffed-side up.
8. Close and lock the lid.
9. Select MANUAL, and then 5 minutes on HIGH pressure.
10. When time is up, press CANCEL and quick-release. Serve with the sauce.

Nutritional Info (per serving): Calories – 209; Fat – 11; Fiber – 2; Carbs – 18; Protein – 10

Brussels Sprouts (VEG, S&F)

(Prep + Cook Time: 5 minutes | Servings: 4)

Cooking Brussels sprouts is not tricky. However, if you overcook them, they will lose their nutritional benefits. So it's best to steam them for a short time. Also, pay attention when cooking them – don't let them sit too long in the pot or they will get mushy.

Ingredients:

1 pound Brussels sprouts

¼ cup pine nuts

Salt and pepper

Olive oil

1 cup water

Directions:

1. Pour the water into the Instant Pot. Set the steamer basket.
2. Put the Brussels sprouts into the steamer basket.
3. Close and lock the lid. Press the MANUAL button. Set the pressure to HIGH and set the time to 3 minutes.
4. When the timer beeps, turn the valve to quick release the pressure.
5. Transfer the Brussel sprouts into a serving plate, season with olive oil, salt, pepper, and sprinkle with the pine nuts.

Note: To prepare the Brussels sprouts, wash them and remove the outer leaves. If some of them are quite large, cut those in half for uniformity - so that they will cook evenly. You will also have to wash the silicone ring of your Instant Pot well after cooking this dish since they can get rather smelly. Soak the ring in dish soap with baking soda and then dry on the counter.

Nutritional Info (per serving): Calories – 106; Fat – 6.2; Fiber – 4.6; Carbs – 11.4; Protein – 5

Eggplant With Carrots, Tomatoes, and Bell Peppers

(Prep + Cook Time: 30 minutes | Servings: 4)

This eggplant dish is nourishing and delicious. It makes a great alternative for meat. Each serving is very low in saturated fat, has no cholesterol, low in sodium, high in manganese, magnesium, and vitamin E.

Ingredients:

1 eggplant, chopped

1 onion, chopped

2 bell peppers,

1 green,

1 red, deseeded and chopped

1-2 tomatoes, chopped

2 carrots, peeled and chopped

1-2 fresh garlic cloves

Salt and pepper

Olive oil, for sautéing

Directions:

1. Prepare all the vegetables and chop them. You can use a vegetable chopper to do this.
2. Set the Instant Pot to SAUTE. Grease the bottom of the inner pot with olive oil. Add the onions, carrots, and tomatoes.
3. Sauté until slightly browned. Add the remaining ingredients, except for the garlic cloves.
4. Add the tomato sauce and then the spices.
5. Set the pot to MANUAL and the timer for 10 minutes.
6. When the timer beeps, quick release the pressure or release the pressure naturally.
7. Serve and enjoy.

Nutritional Info (per serving): Calories – 78; Fat – 0.5; Fiber – 6.6; Carbs – 18.3; Protein – 2.6

Spaghetti Squash (VEG)

(Prep + Cook Time: 20 minutes | Servings: 4)

Spaghetti squash is a refreshing and healthy substitute for pasta. The noodle-like strands in squash have mild and delicate flavor with a light crunch.

Ingredients:
1 whole winter squash
8 fluid oz water, chilled

Directions:
1. Cut squash in half lengthwise and remove and discard seeds using a spoon.
2. In the Instant Pot pour water and then insert a steamer basket.
3. Place squash halves in the steamer and secure pot with lid. Then position pressure indicator and adjust cooking time on timer pad to 6 minutes and let cook until done.
4. When the timer beeps, switch off the Instant Pot and do a quick pressure release.
5. Then uncover the pot, transfer squash from the pot and gently pull of the flesh from the skin as strands using a fork.
6. Serve squash spaghetti immediately.

Nutritional Info (per serving): Calories – 178; Fat – 3.3; Fiber – 1.2; Carbs – 39.7; Protein – 98

Sweet and Sour Red Cabbage (VEG)

(Prep + Cook Time: 35 minutes | Servings: 4)

Serve this recipe as a side dish with pirogues or serve with some baked tempeh or tofu. You can also wrap some chopped potato with foil, add it on top of the cabbage, and cook with the cabbage to make mashed potatoes. Adjust the sweetness and sourness depending on your preference.

Ingredients:
For the sauté ingredients:
4 cloves garlic, minced
½ cup onion, minced
1 tbsp mild oil, OR use broth for oil-free
For the Instant Pot:
1 cup water
1 cup applesauce
1 tbsp apple cider vinegar
6 cups cabbage, chopped
Salt and pepper, to taste

Directions:
1. Press the SAUTE key of the Instant Pot and select the NORMAL option for medium heat.
2. Add the oil/ broth into the pot. Add the onion and sauté until they become transparent. Add the garlic and sauté 1 minute.
3. Add the Instant Pot ingredients. Press the CANCEL key to stop the sauté function. Cover and lock the lid. Press the MANUAL key, set the pressure to HIGH, and set the timer for 10 minutes.
4. When the Instant Pot timer beeps, press the CANCEL key. Using an oven mitt or a long handled spoon, turn the steam valve to quick release the pressure.
5. Unlock and carefully open the lid. Serve.

Nutritional Info (per serving): Calories – 104; Fat – 3.7; Fiber – 4.6; Carbs – 17.5; Protein – 2.2

Ratatouille (VEG)

(Prep + Cook Time: 30 minutes | Servings: 8)

Ratatouille is usually sautéed on the stovetop or baked in the oven. Now, you can cook it in your Instant Pot. This dish tastes even better the next day so you can make it ahead of time and serve it at room temperature.

Ingredients:

4 small zucchini, sliced thin
2 small eggplants, peeled and then sliced thin
1 can (28 oz) crushed tomatoes
1 jar (12 oz) roasted red peppers, drained and sliced
1 medium onion, sliced thin
1 tbsp olive oil
1 tsp salt
2 cloves garlic, crushed
½ cup water

Directions:

1. With the slicing disk of a food processor, prepare the zucchini, eggplant, and onion.
2. Alternatively, you can slice them thin by hand. Press the SAUTE button of the Instant Pot.
3. Put the olive oil in and heat until shimmering.
4. Add the vegetables and sauté for 3 minutes or until they start to soften.
5. Season with the salt and then add the crushed tomatoes and the water; stir to combine.
6. Close and lock the lid. Press the MANUAL button of the pot. Set the pressure to HIGH and set the timer to 4 minutes.
7. When the timer beeps, turn the steam valve to quick release the pressure.
8. Serve immediately. If there are any leftovers, you can store in the refrigerator for up to 5 days.

Nutritional Info (per serving): Calories – 116; Fat – 2.2; Fiber – 9.5; Carbs – 22.1; Protein – 5

Polenta with Fresh Herbs (VEG)

(Prep + Cook Time: 20 minutes | Servings: 6)

Polenta can be tricky to get just right, but it's easy when you use the Instant Pot. This is a simple recipe with simple, rustic flavors coming from lots of fresh herbs, onion, and garlic. You can use dried; just remember to reduce the amount by about half, since dried herbs have more concentrated flavor.

Ingredients:

4 cups veggie broth
1 cup coarse-ground polenta
½ cup minced onion
1 bay leaf
3 tbsp fresh, chopped basil
2 tbsp fresh, chopped Italian parsley
2 tsp fresh, chopped oregano
2 tsp minced garlic
1 tsp fresh, chopped rosemary
1 tsp salt

Directions:

1. Preheat your cooker and dry-sauté the onion for about a minute.
2. Add the minced garlic and cook for one more minute.
3. Pour in the broth, along with the oregano, rosemary, bay leaf, salt, half the basil, and half the parsley. Stir.
4. Sprinkle the polenta in the pot, but don't stir it in. Close and seal the lid.
5. Select MANUAL and cook on high pressure for 5 minutes.
6. When the timer beeps, press CANCEL and wait 10 minutes.
7. Pick out the bay leaf. Using a whisk, stir the polenta to smooth it.
8. If it's thin, simmer on the SAUTE setting until it reaches the consistency you like.
9. Season to taste with salt and pepper before serving.

Nutritional Info (per serving): Calories – 103; Fiber – 2; Carbs – 3; Protein – 0

Mushroom Gravy (VEG)

(Prep + Cook Time: 45 minutes | Servings: 4)

This vegetarian gravy is rich in the flavors of white mushrooms. Serve it with everything.

Ingredients:

2 tbsp olive oil
8 oz sliced white mushrooms
4 tbsp all-purpose flour
4 tbsp vegan butter
2 fluid ounce vegetable broth
2 fluid ounce almond milk
22 fluid ounce water

Directions:

1. Plug in and switch on the Instant Pot, select SAUTE option, add oil and let heat.
2. Then add mushrooms and cook for 5-7 minutes or until nicely golden brown.
3. Pour in broth and continue cooking until mushrooms turn into dark color.
4. Press CANCEL, then pour in water and stir until just mixed. Secure pot with lid, then position pressure indicator, select MANUAL option and adjust cooking time on timer pad to 5 minutes and let cook.
5. Instant Pot will take 10 minutes to build pressure before cooking timer starts.
6. When the timer beeps, switch off the Instant Pot and let pressure release naturally for 10 minutes and then do quick pressure release.
7. Then uncover the pot and drain mushrooms and return to the pot, reserve broth.
8. Place a medium-sized saucepan over medium heat, add butter and let heat until melt completely.
9. Then gradually stir in flour and then slowly whisk in reserved broth until combined.
10. Pour in milk, stir in mushrooms and bring the mixture to simmer, whisk occasionally.
11. Simmer mixture for 8 minutes until gravy reaches desired thickness and then ladle into serving platters. Serve immediately.

Nutritional Info (per serving): Calories – 64; Fat – 0.79; Fiber – 1; Carbs – 12.69; Protein –2

Broccoli Pesto (VEG)

(Prep + Cook Time: 20 minutes | Cups: 2 ½)

Pesto is usually made with just basil and pine nuts, but for something a little different, there's this broccoli pesto with walnuts. If you don't care for basil, the broccoli provides a milder flavor, and goes great with pasta.

Ingredients:

1 pound broccoli florets
3 cups water
3 minced garlic cloves
1 cup fresh basil leaves
⅓ cup toasted walnuts
¼ cup olive oil
¼ cup grated Parmesan
2 tbsp lemon juice
Salt + pepper

Directions:

1. Add broccoli and water to Instant Pot.
2. Press MANUAL and cook for 3 minutes on HIGH pressure.
3. While that cooks, pulse walnuts and garlic in a food processor.
4. When crumbly, stop.
5. When the pot timer goes off, press CANCEL.
6. Quick-release the pressure. Take out the broccoli and rinse in cold water.
7. Drain and pulse in the food processor with oil, basil, and lemon juice.
8. Pulse and add ¼ cup of cooking liquid, cheese, salt, and pepper.
9. Keep pulsing until smooth, adding cooking liquid if needed.
10. Serve with pasta.

Nutritional Info (per serving): Calories – 248; Fat – 3; Fiber – 4; Carbs – 10; Protein – 9

Sweet And Sour Red Cabbage (VEG)

(Prep + Cook Time: 40 minutes | Servings: 4)

Serve this recipe as a side dish with pierogis or serve with some baked tempeh or tofu. You can also wrap some chopped potato with foil, add it on top of the cabbage, and cook with the cabbage to make mashed potatoes. Adjust the sweetness and sourness depending on your preference.

Ingredients:

For the sauté ingredients:

4 cloves garlic, minced

½ cup onion, minced

1 tbsp mild oil, OR use broth for oil-free

For the Instant Pot:

1 cup water

1 cup applesauce

1 tbsp apple cider vinegar

6 cups cabbage, chopped

Salt and pepper, to taste

Directions:

1. Press the SAUTE key of the Instant Pot and select the NORMAL option for medium heat.
2. Add the oil/ broth into the pot. Add the onion and sauté until they become transparent.
3. Add the garlic and sauté 1 minute.
4. Add the Instant Pot ingredients. Press the CANCEL key to stop the sauté function. Cover and lock the lid.
5. Press the MANUAL key, set the pressure to HIGH, and set the timer for 10 minutes.
6. When the Instant Pot timer beeps, press the CANCEL key.
7. Turn the steam valve to quick release the pressure. Unlock and carefully open the lid. Serve.

Nutritional Info (per serving): Calories – 104; Fat – 3.7; Fiber – 4.6; Carbs – 17.5; Protein – 2.2

Stocks and Sauces

Chicken Stock

(Prep + Cook Time: 120 minutes | Liters: 4)

If you use chicken stock all the time, then you need to start making your own stock. – Whether you use it as a base or in soups, homemade broths and stocks are healthier than store bought ones. They are low in sodium and you can tweak the flavor to suit your taste.

Ingredients:

1 chicken carcass

1 onion, cut into quarters

10-15 whole pieces peppercorns

2 bay leaves

2 tbsp apple cider vinegar

Veggie scraps, optional

Water Equipment: 4-5 mason jars

Directions:

1. Put the chicken carcass in the Instant Pot. If desired, feel free to add the skin.
2. Add the vegetable scraps, onion, apple cider vinegar, peppercorns, and bay leaves.
3. Fill the pot with water to 1/2-inch below the max line. Cover and lock the lid. Press the SOUP key and set the timer for 120 minutes.
4. When the Instant Pot timer beeps, press the CANCEL key and unplug the Instant Pot. Let the pressure release naturally for 10-15 minutes or until the valve drops – do not turn the steam valve for at least 30 minutes. Turn the steam to release remaining pressure.
5. Unlock and carefully open the lid. Strain out everything else from the stock and discard.

6. Put a funnel over a mason jar. Pour the stock into the mason jar – do not overfill. If you are planning to freeze your stock, use 5 mason jars.
7. Let the stock cool and then store in the fridge or freeze within 3 days.

Note: Let the jars cool completely before putting them in the fridge or freezing them. If not freezing, be sure to use in 3 days. If not using within 3 days, then freeze.

Nutritional Info (per serving): Calories – 162; Fat – 5.8; Fiber – 0; Carbs – 3.9; Protein – 20.5

Beef Bone Broth

(Prep + Cook Time: 90 minutes | Servings: 8)

The Instant Pot is indeed the answer for your bone broth cooking. With just 90 minutes to cook a batch, you can cook multiple batch a day to make stocks that will last you for more than 2 to 3 months. For the best broth, choose cuts that are filled with cartilage, such as beef oxtail or neck bones.

Ingredients:

5 ounces carrots

4-5 sprigs thyme

4 cloves garlic

3 pounds beef bones (oxtail or neck bones preferred)

3 bay leaves

1 onion, roughly chopped

Half head celery, chopped

Pepper, to taste Salt, to taste

Directions:

1. Cut the celery and onion. Add into the Instant Pot. Add the rest of the ingredients into the pot.
2. Fill the pot with water up to the line before the max line of the Instant Pot.
3. Cover and lock the lid. Turn the steam valve to SEALING. Press the MANUAL key, set the pressure to HIGH, and set the timer for 90 minutes.
4. When the Instant Pot timer beeps, press the CANCEL key and unplug the Instant Pot. Turn the steam valve to quick release the pressure.
5. Unlock and carefully open the lid. Strain the broth and store in freezer.

Bone Broth

(Prep + Cook Time: 1 hour 40 minutes | Servings: 8)

Homemade broths are budget-friendly. Regular consumption of bone broth is also good for your health. They contain minerals, such as sulfur, silicon, phosphorus, magnesium, calcium, and other trace minerals, in their easily absorbed form. They also contain nutrients that support joint function, chondroitin and glucosamine, that are expensive supplements.

Ingredients:
1 tsp unrefined sea salt
1-2 tbsp apple cider vinegar
2-3 pounds bones (2-3 pounds lamb, beef, pork, or non-oily fish, or 1 carcass of whole chicken)
Assorted veggies (1/2 onion, a couple carrots, a couple stalks celery, and fresh herbs, if you have them on hand)
Filtered water

Directions:
1. Put the bones in the Instant Pot. Top with the veggies. Add the salt and apple cider vinegar.
2. Pour in enough water to fill the pot 2/3 full.
3. If you have enough time, let the pot sit for 30 minutes to allow the vinegar to start pulling the minerals out of the bones.
4. Cover and lock the lid. Press the SOUP key, set the pressure to LOW, and set the timer for 120 minutes.
5. When the Instant Pot timer beeps, press the CANCEL key and unplug the Instant Pot. Let the pressure release naturally for 10-15 minutes or until the valve drops.
6. Unlock and carefully open the lid. Strain the broth.
7. Discard the veggies and bones. Pour the broth into jars. Store in the refrigerator or freeze.

Note: If you are using pork, lamb, or beef bones, roast them in a preheated 350F oven for 30 minutes. This step is optional, but it does wonders to the flavors of the broth.

Meat Sauce

(Prep + Cook Time: 15 minutes | Servings: 4)

Cooking meat sauce has never been so easy. Each serving is high in niacin, selenium, and zinc, and very high in iron, vitamin B6, and vitamin B12. Serve with your favorite cooked pasta.

Ingredients:

1 can Hunts traditional pasta sauce
1 pound extra-lean ground beef
¼ cup fresh parsley, chopped
3-4 cloves garlic, minced
3-4 fresh basil leaves, chopped

Directions:

1. Put all of the ingredients into the Instant Pot. With a spatula, break the meat up and mix to combine.
2. Cover and lock the lid. Press the MANUAL key, set the pressure to HIGH, and set the timer for 8 minutes.
3. When the Instant Pot timer beeps, press the CANCEL key and unplug the Instant Pot. Turn the steam valve to quick release the pressure.
4. Unlock and carefully open the lid.

Nutritional Info (per serving): Calories – 363; Fat – 11.7; Fiber – 4.6; Carbs – 24.4; Protein – 37.7

Vegetable Stock (VEG)

(Prep + Cook Time: 30 minutes | Cups: 8)

Veggie stock is super easy to make, and the ingredients are cheap. All you need are the Big Four aromatics - onion, carrots, celery, and a bay leaf - and peppercorns. That bay leaf adds just a teeny bit of that herbal spiciness.

Ingredients:

2 green onions, sliced

2 tsp minced garlic

4 medium-sized carrots, peeled and chopped

4 celery stalks, chopped

6 parsley sprigs

4 thyme sprigs

1,8 liters water

2 bay leaves

8 black peppercorns

1½ tsp salt

Directions:

1. Prepare vegetables. In a 6-quarts Instant Pot, pour in water and add all the ingredients except salt.
2. Plug in and switch on the Instant Pot, and secure pot with lid.
3. Then position pressure indicator, press SOUP option, and adjust cooking time to 30 minutes and let cook. Instant Pot will take 10 minutes to build pressure before cooking timer starts.
4. When the timer beeps, switch off the Instant Pot and let pressure release naturally for 10 minutes and then do quick pressure release.
5. Then uncover the pot and pass the mixture through a strainer placed over a large bowl to collect stock and vegetables on the strainer.
6. Stir salt into the stock and let cool completely before storing or use it later for cooking.

Tomato Sauce (VEG)

(Prep + Cook Time: 50 minutes | Cups: 8)

Making tomato sauce using fresh tomatoes can be is fuzzy when doing it the traditional way. Cooking it in an Instant Pot is more efficient and will take less dishes to wash afterwards.

Ingredients:
4.2 pounds tomatoes, cut into halves or quarters, less or more to fill the Instant Pot to the max level
1 onion, minced
1 tbsp oregano
1 tbsp salt
1 tbsp sugar
2 bay leaves
2 tbsp basil, chopped
2-3 tbsp parsley, chopped
Lemon juice (1 tbsp per jar)

Directions:
1. Put all of the ingredients in the Instant Pot. Cover and lock the lid. Press the MANUAL key, set the pressure to HIGH, and set the timer for 30-40 minutes.
2. While the sauce is cooking, sterilize the mason and new lids in a pot of boiling water for 15 minutes.
3. Drain the sterilized jars and lids on a paper towel.
4. When the Instant Pot timer beeps, press the CANCEL key and unplug the Instant Pot. Let the pressure release naturally for 10-15 minutes or until the valve drops.
5. Unlock and carefully open the lid. Set a food mill over another pot.
6. Scoop out the tomatoes into the food mill. The tomatoes will mush up quickly and go through the pot, leaving the seeds and the skins behind.
7. Put 1 tablespoon lemon juice or 1/4 teaspoon citric acid on each mason jar and immediately fill the mason jars with the hot sauce.
8. Wipe the rims to ensure that the lids will seal. Put the lids on and screw them down.
9. Put the jars in the boiling water where you sterilized the jars and rims. Sterilize for 30 minutes.
10. Remove the jars and let them cool – make sure that each lid pops and is concave.

Nutritional Info (per serving): Calories – 60; Fat – 0.7; Fiber – 3.5; Carbs – 12.9; Protein – 2.5

Mushroom Sauce (VEG)

(Prep + Cook Time: 15 minutes | Cups: 2)

Ingredients:
10 mushrooms, chopped
1 yellow onion, chopped
2 garlic cloves, minced
1 tsp thyme, dried
2 cups veggie stock
½ tsp rosemary, dried
½ tsp sage
1 tsp sherry
1 tbsp water
1 tbsp nutritional yeast
1 tbsp coconut aminos
Salt and black pepper to the taste
¼ cup almond milk
2 tbsp rice flour

Directions:
1. Set your Instant Pot on SAUTE mode, add onion and brown for 5 minutes.
2. Add mushrooms and the water, stir and cook for 3 minutes.
3. Add garlic, stir again and cook for 1 minute.
4. Add stock, yeast, sherry, soy sauce, salt, pepper, sage, thyme and rosemary, coconut aminos, stir, cover and cook on HIGH pressure for 4 minutes.
5. Meanwhile, in a bowl, mix milk with rice flour and stir well.
6. Release pressure from the pot, add milk mix, stir well, cover and cook on HIGH for 6 more minutes.
7. Relies pressure again and serve sauce.

Cranberry Apple Sauce (VEG)

(Prep + Cook Time: 20 minutes | Cups: 2)

This homemade cranberry sauce is made without high fructose corn syrup or white sugar. It's easy, fast, and delicious.

Ingredients:

1-2 apples, medium-sized, peeled, cored, and then cut into chunks
10 oz cranberries, frozen or fresh, preferably organic
¼ tsp sea salt
¼ cup lemon juice
½ cup maple syrup OR honey OR omit
1 tsp cinnamon

Directions:

1. Put all of the ingredients in the Instant Pot and combine.
2. Cover and lock the lid. Press the MANUAL key, set the pressure to HIGH, and set the timer for 1 minute.
3. When the Instant Pot timer beeps, let the pressure release naturally for 10-15 minutes or until the valve drops. Press the CANCEL key and unplug the Instant Pot.
4. Unlock and carefully open the lid. Using a wooden spoon, mash the fruit a bit.
5. Press the SAUTE key and simmer for 1-2 minutes to allow some of the water to evaporate and the mix to thicken.
6. Press the CANCEL key. If you omitted the maple syrup/ honey and want to sweeten with stevia, then add to taste.
7. Stir to combine. Transfer into a pint jar and refrigerate.

Nutritional Info *(per serving):* Calories – 176; Fat – 0.3; Fiber – 4.3; Carbs – 41.4; Protein – 0.3

Tabasco Sauce

(Prep + Cook Time: 25 minutes | Cups: 2)

Cooking Tabasco in an Instant Pot extracts the flavor and the color from the hot peppers in just one minute of high pressure cooking. This sauce is vivid red, bold, and amazingly bright with heat with the hint of pepper. It mimics the flavor of faded and aged Tabasco sauce.

Ingredients:

12 oz fresh hot peppers OR any kind, stems removed

2 tsp smoked or plain salt

1 ¼ cup apple cider

Directions:

1. Press the SAUTE key of the Instant Pot.
2. Roughly chop the hot peppers and put into the Instant Pot. Pour in just enough vinegar to cover the peppers. Add the salt.
3. Press the CANCEL key to stop the sauté function. Cover and lock the lid. Press the MANUAL key, set the pressure to HIGH, and set the timer for 1 minute.
4. When the Instant Pot timer beeps, press the CANCEL key and unplug the Instant Pot. Let the pressure release naturally for 10-15 minutes or until the valve drops.
5. Using an oven mitt or a long handled spoon, turn the steam valve to release remaining pressure. Unlock and carefully open the lid.
6. Using an immersion blender, puree the contents and strain into a fresh dished-washed or sterilized bottle.
7. Refrigerate for up to 3 months or transfer into a suitable container and freeze for up to 1 year.

Nutrition Information per 1 Tablespoon Serving: Calories – 14; Fat – 0.1; Fiber – 0; Carbs – 3.3; Protein – 0.3

Dessert Recipes

Find the best dessert ideas for your Instant Pot in this chapter. There are fast & easy recipes below.

Apple Crisp

(Prep + Cook Time: 15 minutes | Servings: 4)

This delicious apple crisp takes less than 15 minutes to cook. Each serving of this warm breakfast or topped with ice cream dessert is high in manganese and very high in vitamin B6.

Ingredients:

5 medium sized apples, peeled and then chopped into chunks

4 tbsp butter

¾ cup old fashioned rolled oats

2 tsp cinnamon

¼ cup flour

¼ cup brown sugar

½ tsp salt

½ tsp nutmeg

½ cup water

1 tbsp maple syrup

Directions:

1. Put the apples into the bottom of the Instant Pot container. Sprinkle with nutmeg and cinnamon.
2. Pour in the water and drizzle with the maple syrup.
3. Melt the butter. In a small-sized bowl, mix the butter with the flour, oats, brown sugar, and salt.
4. By spoonful, drop the mix on top of the apples.
5. Close the lid of the pot and make sure the valve is closed. Set to MANUAL, the pressure to HIGH, and the timer to 8 minutes.
6. When the timer beeps, let the pressure release naturally and let sit for a couple of minutes to allow the sauce to thicken.
7. Serve as a warm breakfast.

Note: You can also top this dish with vanilla ice cream and serve as a scrumptious dessert.

Nutritional Info (per serving): Calories – 359; Fat – 13.1; Fiber – 7.9; Carbs – 61.1; Protein – 3.6

Cranberry Apple Steel Cut Oats

(Prep + Cook Time: 50 minutes | Servings: 6)

This delicious oat recipe is low in cholesterol, high in manganese, and very high in vitamin B6. You can add the salt, maple syrup, and the vanilla to soak overnight, if desired; leaving out the salt, some say, makes whole grain more digestible. It works well either way.

Ingredients:
1 ½ cup fresh cranberries (dried cranberries or cherries)
1 cup yogurt (or 1 cup milk or part whey)
1 tsp fresh lemon juice
½ tsp nutmeg
½ tsp salt
¼ cup maple syrup
1-2 tsp cinnamon
2 cups steel cut oats
2-4 tbsp butter and/ or virgin coconut oil
3 cups water
4 apples, diced (or 1-2 cups applesauce)
2 cups milk
2 tsp vanilla (optional)

Directions:
1. Grease the bottom of the Instant Pot container with butter/ oil.
2. Except for the salt, maple syrup, and vanilla, put the rest of the ingredients into the pot; let soak overnight.
3. In the morning, add the salt, maple syrup, and, if using, vanilla; cook on PORRIDGE for about 35-40 minutes. Be sure to close the valve.
4. When the timer beeps, turn the steam valve to quick release the pressure.
5. Serve with your favorite milk.

Note: The Instant Pot will automatically switch to warm and naturally release the pressure when the timer beeps.

Nutritional Info (per serving): Calories – 311; Fat – 8.1; Fiber – 28.3; Carbs – 53.8; Protein – 9

Baked Apples (VEG)

(Prep + Cook Time: 40 minutes | Servings: 6)

If you are not in the mood to make an elaborated dessert, then this recipe is for you.

Ingredients:

6 apples

4 oz white sugar

1 tsp cinnamon powder

1 oz raisins

8 oz red wine

Directions:

1. Rinse and core apple and place in a 6-quarts Instant Pot. Sprinkle with sugar, cinnamon, and add raisins and red wine.
2. Secure pot with lid, then position pressure indicator, select MANUAL option and adjust cooking time on timer pad to 10 minutes and let cook.
3. When the timer beeps, switch off the Instant Pot and let pressure release naturally for 10 minutes and then do quick pressure release.
4. Then uncover the pot and scoop out apples.
5. Serve apples with the cooking liquid.

Nutritional Info (per serving): Calories – 188; Fat – 0.3; Fiber – 3.8; Carbs – 34.7; Protein – 0.6

Carrot Cake Breakfast Oatmeal

(Prep + Cook Time: 25 minutes | Servings: 6)

This warm, hearty oatmeal dish tastes like carrot cake, but heart and eye-healthy with every bite. Each serve is low in cholesterol, very high in manganese, and very high in vitamin A.

Ingredients:

1 cup grated carrots
1 cup steel cut oats
1 tbsp butter
1 tsp pumpkin pie spice
¼ cup chia seeds
¼ tsp salt
2 tsp cinnamon
3 tbsp maple syrup
¾ cup raisins
4 cups water

Directions:

1. Put the butter into the Instant Pot; select SAUTE.
2. When the butter is melted, add the oats; toast, constantly stirring for about 3 minutes or until the oats are nutty.
3. Add the water, carrots, cinnamon, maple syrup, salt, and pumpkin pie spice. Close the lid of the pot. Set the pressure to HIGH and the timer to 10 minutes.
4. When the timer beeps, turn off the pot, let the pressure release naturally for 10 minutes, then turn the steam valve to release remaining pressure.
5. When the valve drops, carefully open the lid. Stir in the oats, chia seeds, and raisins.
6. Close the lid and let sit for about 5-10 minutes or until the oats are cooked in the heat to desired thickness.
7. Serve topped with milk, chopped nuts, and additional raisins and maple syrup.

Note: You can cook a batch ahead of time; just freeze individual portions. When ready to serve, add a bit of milk and serve cold or microwave until heated.

Nutritional Info (per serving): Calories – 159; Fat – 3; Fiber – 2.9; Carbs – 32.9; Protein – 2.6

Lemon-Ruby Pears (VEG)

(Prep + Cook Time: 40 minutes | Servings: 4)

Beautiful Bosc pears are dyed crimson with grape juice and currant jelly that's also been flavored with vanilla and lemon.

Ingredients:

4 ripe Bosc pears

3 cups grape juice

1 cup currant jelly

1 lemon

½ split vanilla bean

Directions:
1. Remove the core from the pears, but leave the top of the pear and stem intact.
2. Pour grape juice and jelly into the Instant Pot.
3. Hit SAUTE and heat until jelly melts.
4. Grate the lemon into the pot, and then squeeze in the juice, as well. Toss in vanilla bean.
5. Cut out four squares of foil, to wrap your pears in. Before wrapping, turn the pears in the cooker sauce.
6. Wrap pears in foil tightly and put in your steamer basket. Insert basket into cooker.
7. Seal the lid. Press MANUAL and adjust to 11 minutes.
8. When the timer beeps, press CANCEL and quick-release the pressure.
9. Unwrap the pears, put in a baking dish, and pour over sauce.
10. Wait till pears are room temperature before storing them in the fridge overnight and then serve!

Nutritional Info (per serving): Calories – 414; Fat –0 ; Fiber – 5.5; Carbs – 109; Protein – 1

Chocolate Cheesecake

(Prep + Cook Time: 2 hours 10 minutes | Servings: 6)

Indulge your family and friends in this cheesy chocolaty goodness.

Ingredients:

12 cups cashews, soaked
5 oz almond flour
2 tbsp coconut flour
2 oz melted coconut oil
½ tsp salt
2/3 cup brown sugar
1 tbsp cocoa powder

3 tsp vanilla extract, divided
2 tbsp honey
4 oz maple syrup
8 fluid ounce almond milk
16 fluid ounce water
2 oz vegan chocolate chips

Directions:

1. Add almond flour, maple syrup and coconut oil in a food processor and pulse until mixture comes together. Blend in 1-2 tablespoons water if the mixture is too dry.
2. Take a 7-inch spring form pan, then spoon oats mixture into it and press into the bottom and a little on the sides.
3. Place pan in a refrigerator until filling is prepared.
4. Drain cashews and reserve their soaking liquid.
5. Add cashew and half of the soaking liquid and pulse until smooth.
6. Then blend in salt, sugar, vanilla and milk and pulse until combined well and pour this mixture into a bowl and then stir in coconut flour and chocolate chip until just mixed.
7. Spoon filling into prepared spring form pan and smooth the top. Pour water in the Instant Pot and insert a trivet.
8. Place prepared spring form pan on the trivet and secure pot with lid.
9. Then position pressure indicator, select MANUAL option and adjust cooking time on timer pad to 55 minutes and let cook.
10. When the timer beeps, switch off the Instant Pot and let pressure release naturally for 10 minutes and then do quick pressure release.
11. Then uncover the pot, carefully remove pan and let the pan cool completely on a wire rack.
12. Chill cake in the refrigerator for 2 hours. Remove outer part of the spring form pan before slicing the cake to serve.

Nutritional Info (per serving): Calories – 321; Fat –19.5 ; Fiber – 7; Carbs – 43; Protein – 14

Cashew-Lemon Cheesecake

(Prep + Cook Time: 4 hours | Servings: 8)

Cheesecake is normally a dessert that's off-limits to vegans. However, when you use ingredients like pureed cashews, almond milk, and dates, you can transform the creamy deliciousness into a totally vegan-friendly treat! Flavored with vanilla, lemon, and fresh raspberries, this cake is refreshingly sweet and summery.

Ingredients:

1 cup oats

½ cup chopped dates (soaked in ¼ cup water for 15-30 minutes)

½ cup walnuts

1 cup soaked cashews (2-4 hours of soak time)

½ cup coconut flour

½ cup sugar

½ cup vanilla almond milk

½ cup fresh raspberries

2 tbsp lemon juice

1 tbsp arrowroot powder

1 tsp vanilla extract

1-2 tsp lemon zest

Directions:
1. Drain your dates, but keep the liquid.
2. Pour 1 ½ cups of fresh water into your Instant Pot and add steamer basket.
3. To make the crust, mix ingredients in the first list in a food processor.
4. If it is too dry and crumbly, add 1 tablespoon of date-liquid until it's right.
5. Your dough should be firm, but not too moist so it's gooey.
6. Press down into a springform pan on the bottom and about an inch up the sides.

7. For the filling, drain the cashews, and keep the water. Add half of this water and cashews into a food processor and pulse until smooth.
8. Add flour, sugar, zest, lemon juice, vanilla, and milk. Blend, add arrowroot, and then blend for one last time.
9. Pour into the pan, using a spatula to smooth the top.
10. Wrap the pan with foil, so the top is covered. Lower into the steamer basket.
11. Close and seal lid.
12. Hit MANUAL and adjust time to 20 minutes on HIGH pressure.
13. When time is up, press CANCEL and wait for the pressure to come down naturally.
14. Carefully remove pan and cool for a little while.
15. Arrange raspberries on the cheesecake and then cool for at least 30 minutes before chilling in the fridge for at least 1 hour.

Nutritional Info (per serving): Calories – 346; Fat – 14; Fiber – 2.6; Carbs – 48; Protein – 10

Cranberry-Pear Cake

(Prep + Cook Time: 55 minutes | Servings: 6)

This simple, steamed cake is moist and studded with fresh pears and cranberries. You can add any fruit you would like, depending on what's in season, so consider this a go-to cake for whenever you need to bring something to a bake sale or to a gathering.

Ingredients:

1 ½ cups water
1 cup chopped pears
½ cup fresh, chopped cranberries
1 ¼ cup whole-wheat flour
½ tsp baking soda
½ tsp baking powder
½ tsp ground cardamom
⅛ tsp salt
½ cup unsweetened almond milk
¼ cup agave syrup
2 tbsp applesauce
2 tbsp ground flax seeds

Directions:

1. Grease a 7-inch bundt pan.
2. Mix dry ingredients in a bowl. Mix wet ingredients in a separate bowl. Mix wet into dry before folding in pears and cranberries.
3. Pour batter into pan and wrap in foil. Pour water into your Instant Pot and lower in trivet or steamer basket. Lower the pan in.
4. Close and seal lid. Select MANUAL and cook on HIGH pressure for 35 minutes.
5. When time is up, press CANCEL and let the pressure come down on its own.
6. Take out the pan and throw away the foil.
7. Cool before serving.

Nutritional Info (per serving): Calories – 163; Fat – 2; Fiber – 2; Carbs – 35; Protein – 4

Stewed Pears (VEG)

(Prep + Cook Time: 40 minutes | Servings: 6)

Steamed pears are infused with flavors of ginger, cinnamon, and its aroma. They are much healthier than the store bought one.

Ingredients:

6 pears, peeled
16 oz brown sugar
1 tsp ground cinnamon
1 tsp ginger powder
4 whole cloves
1 bay leaf
½ cup basil leaves
26 oz red wine

Directions:

1. In the Instant Pot, pour in red wine, then stir in cinnamon, ginger and add cloves and bay leaf. Add pears and secure pot with lid.
2. Then position pressure indicator, select MANUAL option and adjust cooking time on timer pad to 4 minutes and let cook.
3. When the timer beeps, switch off the Instant Pot and let pressure release naturally for 10 minutes and then do quick pressure release.
4. Then uncover the pot and pull out pears and set aside. Turn on the pot, select SAUTE option and simmer cooking liquid or until reduced to one-third of the actual amount.
5. Drizzle pears with its cooking liquid, sprinkle with basil and serve.

Nutritional Info (per serving): Calories – 197; Fat – 0.4; Fiber – 4.3; Carbs – 51; Protein – 0.53

Rich and Creamy Rice Pudding

(Prep + Cook Time: 25 minutes | Servings: 6)

This Instant Pot rice pudding recipe is easy and quick to make. It comes out creamy and rich. Each serving is low in sodium.

Ingredients:

¾ cups rice, medium grain (I used Arborio)

2 ½ cups almond milk

¼ tsp salt

1/3 cup sugar

1/3 cup raisins

½ tsp cinnamon

1 tsp lemon zest

1 tbsp butter

1 egg

Directions:

1. Put the rice, milk, salt, and sugar into the Instant Pot. Stir to mix.
2. Press the SAUTE key of the Instant Pot and bring the mix to a boil while constantly stirring.
3. When the mixture is boiling, Press the CANCEL key to stop the sauté function. Cover and lock the lid.
4. Press the RICE key and let cook on automatic time.
5. Meanwhile, whisk the egg with the vanilla.
6. When the Instant Pot timer beeps, press the CANCEL key and unplug the Instant Pot. Let the pressure release naturally for 15 minutes.
7. Unlock and carefully open the lid.
8. Add the egg mixture, butter, raisins, lemon, and cinnamon. Stir to mix.
9. Serve warm or chill in the fridge before serving. If desired, sprinkle with cinnamon on top.

Nutritional Info (per serving): Calories – 408; Fat – 26.7; Fiber – 2.9; Carbs – 41.8; Protein – 5.1

Pears Stewed in Red Wine (VEG)

(Prep + Cook Time: 15 minutes | Servings: 6)

This dessert is tart and sweet at the same time. These wine stewed pears are a stunning treat. Each serving is high in fiber and manganese.

Ingredients:

6 pears, firm ripe, peeled
4 cloves (the spice)
2 cups sugar, optional
1 stick cinnamon OR
1 tsp cinnamon
1 piece fresh ginger OR
1 tsp ginger
1 bunch herbs, for decoration - mint, sage, basil, or oregano
1 bottle red wine (something dry, tarty, and tannic)
1 bay laurel leaf

Directions:

1. Peel the pears – leave the stem attached. Pour the bottle of wine into the Instant Pot.
2. Add the sugar, ginger, cinnamon, cloves, and bay. Mix well until the sugar is dissolved.
3. Add the pears into the pot. Cover and lock the lid.
4. Press the MANUAL key, set the pressure to HIGH, and set the timer for 5-7 minutes.
5. When the Instant Pot timer beeps, press the CANCEL key. Let the pressure release naturally for 10 minutes.
6. Unlock and carefully open the lid. Using 2 spoons or tongs, carefully pull out the pears from the pot.
7. Transfer them onto a plate and set aside. Press the SAUTE key.
8. Cook the cooking liquid until reduced to a third of its original amount.
9. Drizzle the syrup over the pears, decorate with some herbs, and serve at room temperature or chilled.

Nutritional Info (per serving): Calories – 232; Fat – 0.6; Fiber – 7.4; Carbs – 36.8; Protein – 1

Mango Cake

(Prep + Cook Time: 50 minutes | Servings: 8)

Mango syrup is usually added into cocktails and other drinks, but in this recipe, it's used as a sweet and fruity flavoring for a moist, fresh-tasting dessert. If you are in charge of a dessert for an event during the summer, this is a great option that's light and fluffy.

Ingredients:

1 ¼ cups flour
¾ cup milk
½ cup sugar
¼ cup coconut oil
1 tbsp lemon juice
1 tsp mango syrup
1 tsp baking powder
¼ tsp baking soda
⅛ tsp salt

Directions:

1. Grease a baking pan that will fit in your Instant Pot.
2. Mix the sugar, oil, and milk in a bowl until the sugar has melted.
3. Pour in mango syrup and mix again.
4. Pour all the dry ingredients through a sieve into the wet.
5. Add lemon juice and mix well.
6. Pour into the baking pan.
7. Pour 1 cup of water into the Instant Pot and lower in a trivet.
8. Lower the baking pan into the cooker and close the lid.
9. Select MANUAL, and cook on high pressure for 35 minutes.
10. When time is up, press CANCEL and wait for the pressure to come down naturally.
11. Check the cake for doneness before cooling for 10 minutes.
12. Serve!

Nutritional Info (per serving): Calories – 230; Fat – 7; Fiber – 0; Carbs – 39; Protein – 2

Chocolate Fondue

(Prep + Cook Time: 5 minutes | Servings: 4)

If you're a chocoholic, fondue is the ultimate guilty pleasure. This recipe only needs two ingredients - chocolate and cream - and because the Instant Pot is so powerful, it only takes two minutes. Serve with fresh fruit and/ or fancy cookies.

Ingredients:
3.5 ounces of dark chocolate (minimum 70% cocoa)
3.5 ounces of cream

Directions:
1. Pour two cups of water into the Instant Pot and lower in the trivet.
2. Put chocolate chunks in a ceramic, heat-proof container that fits into the pressure cooker, and pour over the cream.
3. Put into the Instant Pot, uncovered.
4. Close the lid and select MANUAL, then adjust time to 2 minutes on HIGH pressure.
5. When time is up, press CANCEL and carefully quick-release.
6. Open the lid and remove the container.
7. Whisk quickly until the chocolate becomes smooth.
8. Serve!

Note: If you want to make your fondue unique, add 1 teaspoon of Amaretto liquor before closing up the pressure. Other flavor options include chili powder, peppermint extract, orange extract, or Bailey's.

Nutritional Info (per serving): Calories – 216; Fat – 20.3; Fiber – 2.6; Carbs – 11.7; Protein – 1.8

Blueberry Pudding

(Prep + Cook Time: 55 minutes | Servings: 4)

This pudding is almost like a little cake packed with fresh blueberries. It's great on its own or with chilled, homemade whipped cream. Read closely, since this recipe is a little different - you actually just steam the pudding for 15 minutes before bringing the cooker to pressure.

Ingredients:

½ pound blueberries
1 cup flour
1 beaten egg
5 ounces milk
½ cup white sugar
½ cup cubed butter
2 ½ tbsp breadcrumbs
1 ½ tsp baking powder
½ tsp salt

Directions:

1. Grease a 4-6 cup pudding basin, or baking dish. In a large bowl, sift in the baking powder, salt, and flour.
2. Add the butter by "cutting" it in, which means using two knives until you get a crumbly, mixed texture.
3. Mix in the breadcrumbs and sugar.
4. Add milk and egg, blending together, before adding blueberries.
5. Pour into your baking dish ¾ of the way full.
6. Cover the top of the dish with a piece of buttered parchment paper, tying with some kitchen string so it stays secured.
7. The paper should have a little pleat in it, so when the pudding rises, it has room.
8. Pour 2-inches worth of hot water in your cooker and lower in the trivet.
9. Put the dish on top and close - not seal - the lid. You're going to just STEAM the pudding for 15 minutes.
10. When that time has passed, now seal the lid.
11. Select MANUAL and cook for 35 minutes on HIGH pressure.
12. When time is up, press CANCEL and quick-release.
13. Take out the pudding and cool for a few minutes before inverting on a plate.

Nutritional Info (per serving): Calories – 493; Fat – 2; Fiber – 0; Carbs – 60; Protein – 8

Pumpkin-Spice Brown Rice Pudding with Dates (VEG)

(Prep + Cook Time: 65 minutes | Servings: 6)

Instead of white rice, we go with brown rice, which has more nutrients like fiber and protein. To up the creaminess factor, there's pumpkin puree, and your pudding ends up tasting like pumpkin pie.

Ingredients:

3 cups almond milk
1 cup pumpkin puree
1 cup brown rice
1 stick cinnamon
½ cup maple syrup
½ cup water
½ cup chopped pitted dates
1 tsp vanilla extract
1 tsp pumpkin spice
⅛ tsp salt

Directions:

1. Pour boiling water over your rice and wait at least 10 minutes.
2. Rinse. Pour milk and water in your Instant Pot.
3. Turn on cooker to SAUTE and when boiling, add rice, cinnamon, salt, and dates.
4. Close and seal lid. Hit MANUAL and cook on HIGH pressure for 10 minutes.
5. Hit CANCEL when the timer goes off and wait for the pressure to descend naturally.
6. Add pumpkin puree, maple syrup, and pumpkin spice.
7. Turn SAUTE back on and stir for 3-5 minutes until thick. Turn off cooker.
8. Pick out cinnamon stick and add vanilla. Move pudding to a bowl and cover in plastic wrap, so the plastic touches the top.
9. Wait 30 minutes to cool. Serve warm or chilled.

Nutritional Info (per serving): Calories – 193; Fat – 3; Fiber – 4; Carbs – 38; Protein – 1

Tapioca with Fresh Berries (VEG)

(Prep + Cook Time: 20 minutes | Servings: 4)

A good dessert (or breakfast, if you need a treat) for vegans. To serve, you layer the pudding with fresh berries, or if you're in a hurry, just mix in the berries and devour.

Ingredients:
2 cups almond milk
2 cups fresh berries
½ cup small pearl tapioca
¼ cup organic sugar
1 tsp pure vanilla

Directions:
1. Rinse tapioca under cold water for half a minute.
2. Pour milk into the Instant Pot, and then add the tapioca.
3. Stir and seal the lid. Hit MANUAL and cook for 4 minutes.
4. When time is up, hit CANCEL and wait 10 minutes before quick-releasing leftover pressure.
5. Mix in sugar and vanilla. To make it a parfait, spoon 2 tablespoons of berries in a glass, followed by tapioca, and then berries, and so on.
6. Serve.

Nutritional Info (per serving): Calories – 180; Fat – 2; Fiber – 1; Carbs – 39; Protein – 2

Made in the USA
San Bernardino, CA
20 December 2017